T0113856

# Love Never Fails

*God loves us all and*
*His love is constant*

KAREN MARIE WATNEY

WESTBOW
PRESS®
A DIVISION OF THOMAS NELSON
& ZONDERVAN

WestBow Press books may be ordered through booksellers or by contacting:

WestBow Press
A Division of Thomas Nelson & Zondervan
1663 Liberty Drive
Bloomington, IN 47403
www.westbowpress.com
844-714-3454

Unless otherwise noted, scripture taken from the New King James Version®. Copyright © 1982 by Thomas Nelson. Used by permission. All rights reserved.

Scripture quotations marked TPT are from The Passion Translation®. Copyright © 2017, 2018, 2020 by Passion & Fire Ministries, Inc. Used by permission. All rights reserved. ThePassionTranslation.com.

ISBN: 978-1-6642-7561-4 (sc)
ISBN: 978-1-6642-7560-7 (e)

Print information available on the last page.

WestBow Press rev. date: 08/31/2022

*Dear Reader,*

*As you read these pages, the most important ingredient will be what God is speaking to your heart. Soak in the truth about what He is saying to you personally. Take time to ponder. You will be glad you did. He is the best Teacher! His words are Life! (John 6:63).*

*This book is sectioned into themes:*

| | |
|---|---|
| *The Father's Love* | *God Loves Me* |
| *I Am Beautiful* | *I Love Me* |
| *1 Corinthians 13:4-8* | *I Love Others* |
| *Prodigal Son Story* | *The Father's Love* |
| *Fruit of the Spirit* | *Love Manifested* |

*Most Scripture verses are taken from the New King James Version. Example: (John 3:16). Some were taken from The Passion Translation. Example: (John 3:16 TPT).*

*Writing these devotions has brought much joy to me! In the process I have learned a lot and experienced the goodness of the Lord.*

*God bless you as you read!*

*Karen Marie Watney*

# The Father's Love ~ God Loves Me!

*How well do you know Father God? What is He like? What does He think of you?*

*The picture you have in your head and in your heart about your Heavenly Father is an important issue in your life! If you have an incomplete or erroneous picture of the Father, you will not walk in the abundant measure of Love, Peace and Joy that is meant for all of us who are children of Father God.*

*Use the scriptures on the pages that follow to further bring understanding of the true nature of our Father. We can also expect the life of Jesus will show us what our Father in heaven is like. Jesus was the image of God. (Colossians 1:15).*

*For us to feel loved is a normal part of our relationship with our heavenly Father. He wants us to know and to experience How Very Much He Loves Us!*

1 John 3:1 Behold what manner of love the Father has bestowed on us, that we should be called children of God!

*Have we not all one Father? Has not one God created us?* (Malachi 2:10).

When Adam and Eve were created, they immediately had a Loving Father. They immediately had a Peaceful Home called The Garden of Eden. The two of them flourished in that atmosphere. They were dependent on their Father, living in fellowship and obedience to Him. Life was good!

After partaking of the forbidden fruit, they hid themselves in fear and shame from the Father. They used fig leaves to cover themselves. All as a result of wanting to "be like God." The most profound result of their disobedience was when they had to leave their Father and their Home. That's when they became orphans.

An orphan is someone who doesn't have a father or a home. Every orphan hopes they will be adopted by a loving family.

We were adopted by Father God! He wanted us; He chose us! We are no longer orphans looking for a place of belonging to feel loved and valued! We are His much-loved children! Part of His great family!

The Father's plan has always been to completely wipe away any "orphan spirit thinking" we may have. The cross demolished the sin barrier between us and the Father. Then, when we were born again, God gave us His Spirit to assure us that we were now part of His Family! We have a loving Father!!

*For you did not receive the spirit of bondage again to fear, but you received the Spirit of adoption by whom we cry out, Abba Father. The Spirit Himself bears witness with our spirit that we are children of God* (Romans 8:15-16).

How many people do you know that do not have good memories of their earthly father? The prisons are full of them; many having no father. Father God wants to be that Father they didn't have. In His Presence He wipes away tears and His love heals hurting hearts. *In Your Presence is fullness of joy* (Psalm 16:11). Father knows how to restore our soul. (Psalm 23:3). Psalm 147:3 TPT says, *He heals the wounds of every shattered heart.*

*My God, My God, why have You forsaken Me?* (Matthew 27:46). Jesus became an orphan in our place on the cross so we don't ever have to be one!

Jeremiah 31:3 The Lord has appeared of old to me saying, "Yes, I have loved you with an everlasting love, therefore with lovingkindness I have drawn you."

Before God made "time" as we know it, the Father's heart was full of love for us. Let that truth sink in! He wants us to know His heart has always been to love us and to never stop loving us. He will not change His mind!

Some of us are better receivers of the Lord's love. The Lord knows our hearts even better than we do. He wants to dialogue with us about hindrances that keep His love at arm's length. His desire is to bring healing to us in those areas. Don't be shy about *committing your soul to a faithful Creator* (1 Peter 4:19). He is the very best heart/soul doctor! The power of His love amazingly heals the most damaged heart.

What we have experienced in our growing-up years can put a hindrance or block to fully embracing the love of the Father. The Lord simply wants us to come to Him for a heart-healing. That's His specialty! Damaged and flawed people are the ones He has! And those are exactly the ones He wants to touch and restore us with His Healing Love. Don't wait until you are perfect to be open with Him about past hurts and pain. He is the "mender of broken hearts" and the "lifter of our heads!" Our God is a tender and gracious Restorer!

How do we see ourselves? Do we use our past to determine our identity? My faults and failings were put onto Jesus on the cross, along with everything I don't like about myself! I am a new creation! (2 Corinthians 5:17). Father stands ready to give me, and all of us, the good things that will replace all negatives. Jesus lives inside of us and He will help us receive the Father's healing love. May our capacity increase to receive the goodness and love He wants to give to us. His love is uplifting and it heals our hurting places. We are drawn to Him because we trust His love wants only the best for us.

What an amazing difference the Father has made in our lives! Where we had anxiety and fear, He replaced it with His peace. Where there was loneliness, He brought comfort and His sweet Presence. When we didn't know what to do next, He showed us the way.

*I will turn their mourning into joy, will comfort them, and make them rejoice rather than sorrow. ...And My people shall be satisfied with My goodness, says the Lord* (Jeremiah 31:13-14). You and I shall be satisfied too!

John 3:16 For God so loved the world that He gave His only begotten Son, that whoever believes in Him should not perish, but have everlasting life.

Every one of us (saint and sinner) has been touched by the amazing love of God! This kind of love is unique because it only comes from God. It wasn't until Jesus demonstrated the God-kind of love with His life, that we have an awareness of how God loves us. The words Jesus spoke and the deeds that He did were done because of love. Jesus shows us the heart of the Father.

God gave for a reason: to have man restored back to Himself. All because of His great love for us, not because we deserved it.

What are some of the characteristics of such an amazing love?

* This kind of love is unconditional, given freely
* It does not depend on the worthiness of the recipient
* It is given to everyone, no one is excluded
* It is a love by choice, an act of the will
* God's love always seeks the highest good for every person

* It does not ask for anything in return, not even a thank you
* This love is known and used in the Christian community

God SO LOVED that HE GAVE. God is telling us by example that Loving and Giving go together! That's one thing we keep in mind when relating to one another. There are many ways to give, not just money. Ask God to let you know the best way to give. Sometimes, it is simply making a phone call. Then you find the person you call has been having a really hard day and is encouraged by your call. Little things mean a lot.

*Whoever believes in God's only Son will not perish, but have everlasting life.* It doesn't take good works or being good enough to earn everlasting life. All it takes is that we pray: "Father God, I'm sorry for my sins, please forgive me. I receive Jesus into my heart and I make Him my Lord."

Are you ready to invite Him into your life? If you are not sure that you will go to Heaven, pray that prayer! That would be the best decision of your life! Don't wait for a better time. God loves you so much! Praying that prayer is the easy part. Jesus did the hard part on the cross, paying for our sins.

*Believe on the Lord Jesus Christ and you shall be saved* (Acts 16:31).

Song of Solomon 2:4 He brought me to the banqueting house and His banner over me was love.

The Father designed a banner with us in mind. A banner is a flag with a message that gives identity to a group of people. When a banner is flown over a group of people, it declares truth about everyone in the group (military, political or religious). A banner is a sign that says those in authority have deemed this truth to be applicable for anyone who has put their trust in that authority. A banner unifies us. Everyone is included under that truth, like being part of the same tribe of people.

The Father's banner over every one of us is LOVE. Our only part is to receive the Father's Love and everything it stands for. We must "own" that truth for ourselves. "God Loves ME! I am a part of God's Love Tribe!"

I can daily declare: "God Loves me - when I am happy and when I'm sad, when I am thankful and when I'm struggling. He loves me when my attitude is upbeat and when my attitude needs help! God loves me ALL THE TIME!" A banner is not taken down every time someone in the group is not living up to what the banner stands for.

Notice that the Lord's banner does not say words like shame, guilt, fear, condemnation, inferior, sorrow or rejection. God defines your life and mine by His Love for us, not by any of the words just mentioned. Our identity, how we see ourselves, should agree with what God has declared over us.

Romans 5:5 tells us, *Now hope does not disappoint, because the love of God has been poured out in our hearts by the Holy Spirit who was given to us.*

We have hope of receiving blessings in the future when we believe our hearts are saturated with the love of God. We don't have to "feel" that love, we simply "believe" that when we were born again we were given the Holy Spirit and He brought God's love with Him!

God demonstrates His love by always seeking our highest and best. He chooses to bless us and doesn't expect us to "be good enough" to receive those blessings. He knows that when His love touches us, we will want to give that love away to others. Since we are so loved, we will want to live pleasing to the Lord. We keep short accounts, repenting when needed.

*We rejoice in salvation, in God's name will set up our banners!* (Psalm 20:5).

## Lamentations 3:23b...Great is Your faithfulness.

## Hebrews 11:11b...Because she (Sarah) judged Him faithful who had promised.

For us to trust the Lord's love for us wholeheartedly, we must believe that He is faithful to be a Promise Keeper! We must know for sure that when we see a promise in the Bible, it is available for us to believe, stand on and take! Sarah bore a child when she was past the age, because she believed that the Promise Maker was Faithful to Make The Promise come to pass!

*God is not a man, that He should lie, nor a son of man that He should change His mind. Has He said, and will He not do? Or has He spoken, and will He not make it good?* (Numbers 23:19).

Our Father God says what He means and means what He says! God has given us exceedingly great and precious promises all through the Bible. It's up to us to stand on those promises! God wants us to write our names on the promises that apply to our situation. That is living by faith. Simply believing that God cannot lie or change His mind brings us into the realm of His supernatural possibilities!

*It is good to give thanks to the Lord, and to sing praises to Your name, O Most High; to declare*

*Your lovingkindness in the morning, and Your faithfulness every night* (Psalm 92:1-2).

Morning is the best time to speak God's Truth out loud to our heart. What we say to ourself and about ourself matters! It will set the tone for the whole day. Say - "Father, I believe You love me with Big Loves! I open my heart to receive Your Love fresh this morning. I'm confident that You will be with me and for me all during the day, no matter the challenges I may face."

Evening is the best time to thank the Lord for His faithfulness to watch over us and to keep us all day! *The Lord is your keeper* (Psalm 121:5). Say - "Father, thank You for committing to be with me all day! I am humbled by Your faithfulness, kindness and care for me. It makes me love You more."

When we experience the mercy and faithfulness of God, especially in trying times, our hearts are filled with rejoicing and worship! *I will sing of the mercies of the Lord forever; with my mouth will I make known Your faithfulness to all generations* (Psalm 89:1).

1 John 4:16 And we have known and believed the love that God has for us. God is love, and he who abides in love abides in God, and God in him.

How do you view God? What is He like? Write down your beliefs about Him. It's good to record what we intellectually believe about God. However, reactions are often a better indicator of beliefs than written proclamations.

Consider the following situations. How would you normally respond to them? How would you respond if you were convinced that God is completely loving, willing to help in any situation?

* Your purse or wallet has been stolen.
* The company you work for has been bought by another firm. Each day someone in your department has lost his/her job. You could be next.
* Think of a problem you have. What would be a normal response and what would be a believing response when you are abiding in God's love?

Is there a discrepancy between what you intellectually believe to be true and how you react under stress?

It is easy for any of us to be immediately moved by feelings. First John 4:16 will help us to catch our breath and tune into truth from God's Word.

The apostle John is telling us to *believe the love God has for us.* This takes determination and practice in the good times, so when the stressful times come, we will have established our faith in God's love for us. No one will ever be able convince us that we are not outrageously loved by our Father in Heaven. As far as we're concerned, we are His favorites!

Next, John talks about those who *abide in love.* There is a difference between visiting a truth and abiding in it! This is where daily reading the Word helps us to feed our heart the truth of God's love. Maybe you would not be able to tell me everything you had for lunch a week ago Thursday, but you did eat and were nourished. The same happens when we are daily in the Word. Our spirit is fed and our beliefs are strengthened.

John says that when we abide in God's love, we can count on the fact that God is in us! Don't look for feelings, stand on the Word that God IS in us!

*As the Father loved Me, I have loved you; abide in My love* (John 15:9).

Psalm 40:17 But I am poor and needy; yet the Lord thinks upon me. You are my Help and my Deliverer; do not delay, O my God.

Remember, it is David, king of Israel, who said, "I am poor!" David was honest with God about how weak he felt at that time. Yet he took comfort in knowing that he was always in God's thoughts. Wow! Do we realize that you and I are always in God's thoughts? I want that same confidence, don't you?

Yet the Lord thinks upon ____. Put your name in there. Tell the Lord HE is your Help and the One who will deliver you from ____ problem. Make this verse personal. Many times in the Psalms, David calls God his Helper!

*God is my Helper...He has delivered me out of all trouble* (Psalm 54:4,7).

Let's become like David, who expected the Lord to be his Help and Deliverer through all the trials of his life. David had a close relationship with His God over many years. He had experienced God's rescue before and knew He would be faithful to be his Deliverer again.

David petitioned the Lord to "not delay!" Perhaps he had a situation that needed immediate attention and his trust was in "my God" to make it right.

How many ways do we need God to help us? What about with finances, with our health, with relationships, with wisdom to make decisions. We need His help in child raising and being good grandparents. We need His help when it comes to planning for our future. He does have a special calling and gifting for each one of us and with His guidance and help along the way He will bring those things into fruition.

Is it possible that we would need His help in our spiritual lives? How about healing the hurts of the past, help to forgive those who have hurt us, and also to forgive ourselves. We need His help to forget about the past and to press on to live for the Lord "in the now!"

What about needing Him to help us pray as we ought, to hear the Father's voice correctly and especially help to deny our flesh and to obey the Spirit.

We give and receive help from those we love and who love us. Father God LOVES us best and HELPS us most! We need God's help in everything!

*I can do all things <u>through Christ</u> who strengthens me* (Philippians 4:13).

Exodus 34:6-7 And the Lord passed
before him (Moses) and proclaimed,
"The Lord, the Lord God, merciful and
gracious...keeping mercy for thousands...

Merciful and gracious! Wow, pretty amazing attributes for a Supernatural Being Who makes galaxies - lots of them! We think of God as being All Powerful, All Knowing and Ever Present. We also know Him as being completely Holy, Pure as blinding Light, not a whisper of darkness in Him.

Exodus 34 relates when Moses was instructed to present himself to God on Mount Sinai. The Lord told Moses who He was - a merciful God!

We can choose to believe that Exodus 34:6 and 7 is really how it is, that God IS merciful. What God claims about His own nature is true and factual and we can count on it for our own lives. Now, as an act of our trust in God's Word, we can receive and enjoy these good things - mercy and grace!

What does mercy look like in real life?

Use your imagination to picture how you would feel, if when you woke up each morning, you knew for sure that God would not be mad at you for the entire day, no matter what messes you may be in or that you caused. What if He was not even mildly upset with you? Ever! That's mercy in action.

How would you feel, if when you woke up, you could actually see the Father standing near your bed and He was smiling? And, He kept smiling over you the whole day! Would that assurance give you a chance to relax, be less prone to be hard on yourself and make you want to chat with the Father all day? That's mercy in action. What a huge blessing from an All-Powerful God!

What does God's mercy mean to you? What it means to me is that I don't have to "do" anything to be a "good enough" person. I simply believe that I am already a good enough person in God's sight because I have been given righteousness as a gift. (2 Corinthians 5:21). The great exchange that took place on the cross: Jesus took our sin and gave us His righteousness. What a trade! That is mercy for sure!

When I think of God's mercy, it doesn't make me think of what I can "get away with," rebelling against His Word.

*...I will trust in the mercy of God forever and ever.* (Psalm 52:8).

## Zephaniah 3:17a The Lord your God in your midst, the Mighty One, will save...

The preceding verse (3:16) paraphrased says, *Don't fear, don't let your hands be weak.* In other words, don't become anxious, don't give up or allow yourself to become discouraged. In difficult times, the prophet Zephaniah is reminding the people of the character of their God.

Zephaniah knew that what the people were putting their focus on was of critical importance. It is the same with us today. Are we looking at negatives or are we looking at what the Bible says about our Lord?

Where we put our focus determines our emotions. How we feel about something is a reaction to what we are thinking about. Do we feel that God is distant, maybe He doesn't know or care about what is going on with us?

Emotions are fickle, they can vary from "up to down" and from "down to up" in a matter of seconds! It all depends on what we believe and think.

Let's determine to believe that what the Bible says is true! And it is true for US! The Lord God is in OUR midst NOW! Even if we don't feel it, the Word says He is near because He loves and cares for us. We are precious to Him!

The Lord our God is called "The Mighty One" for a reason. He is always victorious! What He says goes! He always does the right thing at the right time. We can rest in Him, knowing that all things are possible with Him.

*The Lord will fight for you, and you shall hold your peace* (Exodus 14:14). Our part is to trust our Mighty One, refuse to fear and *Stand still and see the salvation of the Lord* (Exodus 14:13). When God fights, He wins!

Why would the Lord even want to be in our midst? I've sometimes wondered why the Lord would bother to be interested in me and have marveled many times at His patience with me. That's what Love Does! Love cares, Love does not let go, it always believes the best. Love sees a better future.

No one understands you and me like the Father, not even our closest friend or family member. The Father loves us all and enjoys us. Love is why He is mighty for us, defending and protecting. He's given us a powerful promise to strengthen and help us. We can tell ourselves - "The Lord my God, the Mighty One, is in my midst and He will save!" Yay!

2 Thessalonians 3:5 Now may the Lord direct your hearts into the love of God...

The Father wants to be our Guide to help us understand, embrace and enjoy the fullness of His love. He shows us how we can be more open to Him. The Study of God's Word, a lifestyle of Humility, Worship and Prayer are ways our heart can be directed into the Love of God.

Study the <u>Word.</u> Some Bible students like to use the "Law of First Mention." This means the first time an important word is mentioned in the Bible, it holds a key to understanding the word's true meaning. The same verse also provides a foundation for its fuller development in later parts of the Bible.

"Love" is first mentioned in Genesis 22:2: *Then He said, "Take now your son, your only son Isaac, <u>whom you love,</u> and go to the land of Moriah and offer him there as a burnt offering..."* This speaks directly of the love the Father has for His Son, who will become the ultimate sacrificial offering.

Develop a lifestyle of <u>Humility</u> when relating to God and to people. There is no room for arrogance or self-exaltation, especially in the family of God. Father doesn't want us to think ourselves to be above others. *God resists the proud, but gives grace to the humble* (1 Peter 5:5).

<u>Worship</u> draws our attention to God and His love. David began worshipping the Lord when he was a youth caring for his father's sheep. He continued his practice of making worship a priority all of his life. *It is good to give thanks... and sing praises to Your name, O Most High; to declare Your lovingkindness* (Psalm 92:1-2). *Your lovingkindness is better than life* (Psalm 63:3).

<u>Prayer</u> makes us open to God's love. 1 Peter 5:7 says, *Casting all your care upon Him, for He cares for you.* What an amazing exchange! We give Him our worries and because He loves us, He gives us just what we need to see our situation turn from negative to positive! He surely does care for us!

Why is it important to direct our hearts into the love of God? Because of the benefits it will give to us! Most of us have "sandpaper people" who can rub us the wrong way! When we allow God's love to quickly wash the offense away, our hearts stay at peace.

*I will bless the Lord who has given me counsel; my heart also instructs me in the night seasons* (Psalm 16:7).

> John 13:23 Now there was leaning
> on Jesus' bosom one of His
> disciples, whom Jesus loved.

The writer of the gospel of John gave himself the nickname "The Disciple Whom Jesus Loved." In other translations it is "The Beloved Disciple."

Did John have an arrogant attitude? Did he think Jesus loved him more than the other disciples? After all, Jesus had His inner circle of three disciples and John was one of them. During the crucifixion, Jesus even asked John to take care of His mother. Was John boasting, trying to elevate himself?

In John 13:23, John does not name himself as the one who leaned on Jesus. He was not trying to focus attention on himself. Perhaps the opposite it true, that he wanted to make himself anonymous. Instead, he draws the spotlight away from himself and puts it on the very One who dramatically changed his life by loving him unconditionally and completely.

John's heart was like a sponge that soaked up that powerful love. He was telling his readers that they too could experience what he did. Through love, John found the truth of his identity and his purpose. We can do the same! It all starts when we become open to receiving the powerful Love of God.

John was not the only disciple that Jesus loved. He loved them all the same. He washed all of their feet on the night of the Last Supper before His crucifixion. Jesus knew that Judas would betray Him, yet He lovingly washed his feet as well.

Are nicknames important? Name changes and nicknames happen in both the Old and New Testaments. Abram became Abraham and Simon became Peter. Both new names gave new identity and calling. In both cases, the Lord gave the new name, giving weight and authority to that person.

What is your new name? What if you began to be known as "Susie the Beloved" or "Tom the Beloved?" What if you called yourself the same, always adding "the Beloved" after your name? How long would it take for your heart to feel the full impact of that new title?

What would it feel like to BE The Beloved of the Lord? Would your heart say, "I am loved and accepted," rather than feeling like an outsider?

*The beloved of the Lord shall dwell in safety by Him* (Deuteronomy 33:12).

1 Chronicles 16:34 Oh, give thanks
to the Lord, for He is good! For
His mercy endures forever.

Just like the foundation of a building is of critical importance for the stability of the building, so our "foundational beliefs" about God are critically important. How would you describe God to someone who has no knowledge of Him? Think about it. What we hold true about Who He is, and especially Who He is for each one of us, is vital for our spiritual growth.

In the natural, foundations are made to be firm enough to stand on! I stand on these truths about Who God is and therefore, Who He is for me:

God is love - therefore, He always loves me with big loves

God never leaves us - therefore, I can count on Him to be with me

God is good - therefore, whatever comes my way, He turns to good

*All things* _work together_ *for good to those who love God, to those who are the called according to His purpose* (Romans 8:28). In times of hardship, disappointments or being treated wrongly, we may not see a way ahead, but we can assure our hearts that God is good and He will make a way for us.

Some bad things happen simply because we live in a fallen world. We sometimes have more questions than answers. That's when God sustains us with His presence and peace. He gives guidance and wisdom, bringing us into a better future. When we don't understand it all with our head, we can still stand strong and be nourished by His goodness in our heart.

A by-product of a trial is that we have the opportunity for our character to mature and be strengthened. We change to become more like Jesus! We tap into the promises of God and we gain His strength working in us. Worldly ways just fall away, not important anymore. What if we said to our problem: "And, it came to pass - it didn't come to stay!" We trust in God's Word!

We can daily be strengthened by truths of the Bible. Words written there are the most powerful weapons we have to overcome any problem. The goodness of God assures us that He will stand by anything He has said to us. He wants us to take our inheritance! Speak out His promises each day. God spoke and the worlds were formed. We can speak to our mountains!

*I will make darkness light before them, and crooked places straight. These things I will do for them, and not forsake them* (Isaiah 42:16).

Psalm 32:8 I will instruct you and teach you in the way you should go; I will guide you with My eye.

Our Father will teach us, guide us and watch our progress. He is the very best Teacher and the very best Guide! He knows all the right paths our lives should take. His timing is always perfect.

*Then the word of the Lord came to me saying: Oh house of Israel, can I not do with you as this potter? says the Lord. Look, as the clay is in the potter's hand, so are you in My hand, O house of Israel!* (Jeremiah 18:5-6).

Jeremiah speaks of Israel as being clay in the Potter's hands. What God makes of His people depends on their response. The quality of the clay limits what the potter can do with it, so the quality of a people limits what God will do with them. I want to be like moldable clay, don't you? Too long I have tried to figure things out by myself and make plans. That doesn't usually work out so well! I've discovered (over time) that asking the Father what to do, how to think and what attitude to have is the very best!

*The humble He guides in justice, and the humble He teaches His way* (Psalm 25:9).

When the clay is humble, it doesn't tell the Potter how to do His work, it just remains soft and surrendered in His hands. The Potter has perfect plans and the clay is the one that comes out looking beautiful! Each one of us becomes a lovely work of art, skillfully crafted by the Master Potter.

*For I know the thoughts that I think toward you, says the Lord, thoughts of peace and not of evil, to give you a future and a hope* (Jeremiah 29:11).

I love that God thinks of me! I also love that He said he would "give" me a future and a hope. There was no mention of me working out my future. All God wants me to do is to submit to Him and talk things over. *Then you will call upon Me, and go and pray to Me, and I will listen to you* (Jeremiah 29:12). Father God wants a conversation with us!

I am thankful that my Father is my Teacher. I place myself at His feet to learn. I open my spiritual ears to hear Him. I read and ponder His Word.

*I will stay close to you, instructing you and guiding you along the pathway for your life. I will advise you along the way* (Psalm 32:8 TPT).

## 1 John 4:8 He who does not love does not know God, for God is love.

God IS Love! That's Who and What He is! Perfect, pure, wholehearted Love toward us. How amazing is that?! Do we have to be "good enough" to receive His love? How many times have I been overtaken by the "not good enough" feeling! These feelings don't come from the Father because He loves imperfect people. He knows perfect people do not exist! My mistakes cannot stop the love of God. His love is bigger than my failings.

Knowing the truth about the true nature of God is extremely important. And, knowing the truth of how He sees you and me is vital and affects every part of our lives. The bottom line is that God IS Love in all of its characteristics.

Please look at these three words with me: "God Loves Me!" Now, let's say each word, emphasizing them one at a time and defining each word as we do. Our hearts needs to hear this simple declaration!

> GOD loves me! - Ultimate Power and Authority, Life-Giver, Perfect Holiness
> God LOVES me! - God's Love gives the Highest and the Best to everyone
> God loves ME! - Not "the whole world" but personal, just me!

Saying these three words over and over and emphasizing each word separately, helps us to realize the full impact of what John was telling us in 1 John 4:8 when he said, *God Is Love!* This truth has to be deeply ingrained in us. He doesn't give love because it's a nice thing to do, He IS Love!

We can't give away what we don't already have. We must first experience the Love of God for ourselves before we can give it away. *The love of God has been poured out in our hearts by the Holy Spirit who was given to us* (Romans 5:5). Armed with that gift of love, we then can give it away!

1 John 4:8 tells us that if our heart is cold towards people, or even cold towards ourselves, it could be we don't believe the Father loves us because we have blown it. Possibly, it is because we blame God for some hurtful thing that happened in the past. He didn't cause it! (John 10:10).

Since we believe in His love, that means we can also trust in His power.

* He promises to - *be a very present help in trouble* (Psalm 46:1).
* Because He loves us, He will bless and favor us (Psalm 5:12).
* We can be at peace while He fights our battles for us (Exodus 14:14).

Psalm 145:8-9 The Lord is gracious and full of compassion, slow to anger and great in mercy. The Lord is good to all.

Our Father is kind and tenderhearted to those who don't deserve it. He's very patient with the ones who fail Him. He shows us mercy and compassion even on our worst days! His way is to be good to us, no matter what!

When we were children we quickly learned that if we studied well in school, we got good grades. When we obeyed Mom, life was good. Reward and punishment depended on our performance. It is very easy to carry that concept into our relationship with the Father. If I'm good, keep a good attitude and don't kick the cat, He is pleased. When I have a bad attitude, He is upset with me, or at least I think He is.

What if I counted on the fact that the Lord is full of compassion, slow to anger and great in mercy? It would change how I would react to a bad day!

I would go to the Father, all while I am feeling upset. I would tell Him how frustrated I am about stuff and how I need help in knowing how I am to process things. He listens and comforts. He lets me know I am not alone, that I can trust Him to fight my battles for me. Then He reminds me that I am His darling daughter and that He has Big Loves for me!

What a difference there is between feeling frustrated and overwhelmed, and the feeling of being loved, accepted and nurtured back into peace! How good it is to know that I don't have to get my act together to feel like I can freely express myself to my Father. His heart is open to me 24/7.

The Father treats me the same as He would treat Jesus. He loves me with the same love. That love lifts up and enables! That love encourages me greatly! Father tells me who I am in Him. Being upset is not the real me!

There's such a freedom in simply BEING a child of God! It eliminates the striving to measure up by trying to DO the right thing all the time! We can relax, submit ourselves to God and His ways, then expect the Lord to teach us and guide us each day. And He will! (Psalm 32:8).

I remind myself that I don't have to earn God's love and blessings by trying to be a "good Christian." God has made us good Christians by putting us "in Jesus" and "Him in us!" Colossians 3:3 says that *we are hidden with Christ in God.* And, *Christ in you, the hope of glory* (Colossians 1:27).

Psalm 147:3,5-6 He heals the brokenhearted and binds up their wounds (sorrows). Great is our Lord and mighty in power; His understanding is infinite. The Lord lifts up the humble...

Our Lord is great and mighty in power! 2 Peter 3:10 says that there will come a time when *the heavens will pass away with a great noise, and the elements will melt with fervent heat; both the earth and the works in it will be burned up.* Verse 13 adds: *Nevertheless we, according to His promise, look for a new heavens and a new earth in which righteousness dwells.*

That description of the Day of the Lord surely lets us know that our Lord is *mighty in power!* Psalm 147 (above) says God's *understanding is infinite.* To me that indicates He has perfect Wisdom regarding everything. Our God is Powerful, Wise, and He is Love *(The Lord heals the brokenhearted and lifts up the humble).*

Power - Wisdom - Love

What an Awesome God we serve! What a diversity of Greatness! Picture Him functioning in each one of those amazing attributes.

The same <u>Powerful</u> God Who will cause the sun, moon and stars to fall away on The Last Day, is the same God that bends low and kisses the broken hearted on their forehead and tells them that He is there for them, to bring healing to all their hurting places. He's a tender comforter, a wise counselor.

The same God Who has the <u>Wisdom</u> to know exactly when the earth is ready to receive The King of Kings, Jesus, to rule the earth, is the same God that knows everything about your life. He knows the hopes and dreams you have for your future. Not only does He have the knowledge, He has the wisdom to lead you the best way and to open doors of fruitfulness for you.

The same God Who will create a new earth where godly people can live in peace, is the same God Who <u>Loves</u> the humble in the here and now. People in many countries are being persecuted for their faith. The Lord joins with them in their jail cells and refugee camps. He supports and strengthens.

*Blessing and honor and glory and power be to Him who sits on the throne, and to the Lamb, forever and ever!* (Revelation 5:13).

# Psalm 23:1 The Lord is my Shepherd, I shall not want.

Newborn lambs can be rejected by a ewe because it is crippled or weak. This one is called a "bummer lamb." Once the ewe rejects that little one, she will not change her mind. She will kick it away, each time harder, until the lamb wanders off with his head hung low, overcome with rejection. The bummer lamb will soon die without nourishment from the mother, being especially vulnerable in cold weather.

The shepherd picks up the traumatized lamb, knowing it will take a lot of love and attention to save its life. At first the baby lamb is fed often with a bottle, wrapped in a blanket for warmth and held close to the shepherd to hear his heartbeat. The lamb becomes part of the shepherd's family, even being carried around by the shepherd's children! The bummer grows in strength from the bottle, but more important is the inner strength that comes by being nourished with the love of the shepherd and his family.

When the time comes for the lamb to return to the sheep world, he will return as a "bummer lamb" and be kicked away if he approached a ewe with her babies. But this time it didn't affect him because he had the love of the shepherd inside of him. No longer a reject, he was an adopted member of the shepherd's family! He held his head high as if he were royalty! When the shepherd came into the field, the sheep at first would not notice. But the bummer would immediately run straight to the shepherd, jumping up and down enthusiastically, joyfully greeting the one who loved him most!

If you have been rejected, God's love will satisfy the deepest parts of your heart and make negative situations not painful anymore. Love heals! It heals on every level. Love between spouses, between parents and children, and between friends. Living loved by God ourselves and then giving that love to someone else always leads to something life-giving and better.

Do we have to deserve God's love? Only His "good kids" get big doses of His love, right? No, that's not how it works. The only qualification the shepherd makes about a lamb is - does that little one need his love and care? We can all say "yes!" We will gladly accept Your healing love, God!

God's love is meant to be encountered and enjoyed every single day! God's love empowers us and it removes the "rejection arrows" of the past.

*I am the Good Shepherd, and I know My sheep, and am known by My own* (John 10:14). Jesus *loved His own…He loved them to the end* (John 13:1).

1 John 4:10 TPT This is love: He loved us long before we loved Him. It was His love not ours. He proved it by sending His Son to be the pleasing sacrificial offering to take away our sins.

Love looks like something! It looks like a bloody cross. It looks like a pure and innocent man taking the place of, and receiving the punishment for, impure and guilty humanity. It looks like humility, courage and obedience, but most of all, it looks like LOVE. No one has ever loved you and me like the man Jesus Christ!

*Looking unto Jesus, the author and finisher of our faith, who for the joy that was set before Him endured the cross, despising the shame, and has sat down at the right hand of the throne of God* (Hebrews 12:2).

Jesus endured the agony of the cross because He focused on the joy of knowing that you and I would be His and our sins would be taken away.

In the beginning, we were created for daily fellowship with God the Father. Mankind was created to receive and experience the Father's love. Adam and Eve walked and talked with Father in the cool of the day. Those refreshing times made them feel very loved. They both knew that the Father God cared about every detail of their lives.

Picture the day the Father walked the two of them to the edge of The Garden. The worst thing about leaving their paradise would be no more walks with the One who loved them most. I can picture Eve sobbing as she hugged the Father and said goodbye. Tears streamed down Father's face too.

Jesus paid for our "crime of sin" and that means that we went free from all judgment. God poured all of His wrath for sin on Jesus, so He does not have any left for us. What is left for us is the ability to walk and talk with the Father in the cool of the day. Fellowship is what we were made for. Those cherished moments that began in the garden are meant to be experienced by each one of us. Be open for His love to refresh you at deep levels.

God's love is freely available to anyone, anywhere. God does not force His love on anyone. We are the ones to choose whether we want to be like Adam and Eve and experience a loving friendship with God. We can take it or not.

*Jesus knew that His hour had come that He should depart...having loved His own who were in the world, He loved them to the end* (John 13:1).

Zephaniah 3:17b ...He will rejoice over you with gladness, He will quiet you with His love, He will rejoice over you with singing.

Have you ever wondered what the face of the Father looks like? If He will rejoice over you with gladness, that means He must be smiling! Can you imagine what a beautiful singing voice He must have, as He sings a joyful song over you! His eyes must emanate the most tender and powerful love there is. Just one look into those eyes would bring supernatural peace.

Can you picture Father God rejoicing over you? Is that a stretch of the imagination? Try. Our lives are meant to have a two-way conversation with Father, just like in the Garden of Eden. *When You said, Seek My face, my heart said to You, Your face, Lord, I will seek* (Psalm 27:8).

We are told in 2 Corinthians 3:18 that *when we behold the glory of the Lord, we are being transformed into the same image.* Whatever we behold, we become. What a powerful truth that can be applied to any area! What if we made a decision to behold/picture the many ways the Father shows His love to us? Every day, pondering the truth that He rejoices over ME, and sings over ME! Even my heart is quieted by His love! What I behold, I become. What I meditate on transforms my heart.

The Father sings over us joyfully! This is the same emotional reaction that heaven has when one sinner repents. (Luke 15:7). When we get to heaven, perhaps we shall see angels dancing with joy! Did you ever think of that?

*He will quiet you with His love.* When a mother meets the needs of her baby, the little one is satisfied and calmed. That is what happens to our hearts when we experience God's love in never-ending fresh ways. *In quietness and confidence shall be your strength* (Isaiah 30:15).

In Psalm 2:4 we find out that God "laughs!" Since we were created in His image, perhaps we laugh because He does! We sing because He sings! Maybe down deep we feel like the style of music we like best must be His favorite too! What does "rejoicing with gladness" mean to you? Does it mean God dances with joy? Wow, what would that look like? Our amazing Father God has emotions and He gave them to us as well to enjoy!

Jesus prays for us: *My joy may remain in you, and that your joy may be full* (John 15:11). Circumstances may not be good, but we can focus on our good God! *Rejoice in the Lord always. Again I say rejoice!* (Philippians 4:4).

# Jude v21 Keep yourselves in the love of God...

Keeping ourselves aware of and in tune with God's love is "making the main thing the main thing!" For God so loved the world... Everything good started from that premise. All uplifting, beneficial and healing things come to us because God so loves us! His love is the bedrock that we stand on.

God <u>created</u> men and women because He wanted a family to love! It was love for us that sent Jesus to <u>redeem</u> us! When we were born again we were <u>inhabited</u> by God's loving Spirit! We flourish in the atmosphere of love!

Psalm 121 shows God's love for us in various ways:

> v2 Our help comes only from the Lord
> v3 He will not let you stumble or fall
> v4 He is your keeper and He will not slumber nor sleep
> v5 He cares for you and shelters you safely
> v6 He gives you 24-hour protection, both day and night
> v7 He will preserve you when in adversity
> v8 He will be with you now and He'll keep you safe forevermore

As children grow up, it is very important that they feel protected, especially by their father. It makes them feel important and to feel at peace. There's no room for worry because "Daddy is in charge! And, I know Daddy loves me!"

How do we keep ourselves "tuned in" to the love of God? First, we have to know what He is really like! Reading our Bible gives us a good description of the true nature and character of God. Also, take a long look at the person of Jesus. He accurately represented His Father in word and deed.

*He who has seen Me has seen the Father; so how can you say, 'Show us the Father'? Do you not believe that I am in the Father, and the Father in Me? The words that I speak to you I do not speak on My own authority; but the Father who dwells in Me does the works* (John 14:9-10).

How do we keep ourselves in a good relationship with a friend? We share our thoughts and feelings. We can do that with our Father. He already knows everything about us, but I think He enjoys it when we are open-hearted and real with Him. How about singing a worship song to Jesus? He is certainly worthy to receive our thanks and praise! Would He take pleasure in hearing you worship? I think so. Worship opens your heart to His love.

*We love Him because He first loved us* (1 John 4:19).

> 1 John 4:18 There is no fear in love;
> but perfect love casts out fear.

I've noticed in my life and in the lives of friends, that there have been experiences in the past that have prepared us for how we are serving the Lord now. We were in "God's School" all along, usually not even recognizing that. The lessons we went through were not always "fun" however!

Proverbs 29:11 tells us that God does have a future and a hope for us. Since He is a good God, what lies ahead for each one of us is a good plan, a God plan! In the meantime, we must "grow through what we go through!"

How can we ever learn how to overcome difficulties in our lives unless we have had some? How can we learn to "fear not" unless we had something that looked too big and scary for us? Many times my learning has been trial and error because I didn't get it right the first time! That usually results in being more dependent on the Lord to help me through. I count on Psalm 32:8, where God says He will teach us and tell us the best way forward.

How can we help others to go through difficult times if we have not learned some valuable lessons ourselves in those same areas? We put our names on certain verses of scripture and make them our own. We live them out! We make them applicable in a particular circumstance by believing them and speaking them out. Every word of scripture is powerful! (Hebrews 4:12).

I have several of those "go to" verses that I use, but definitely the ones I have used the most over the years have been Isaiah 12:2, *I will trust and not be afraid* and Psalm 56:3, *When I am afraid I will trust in You.*

I picture David as being amazingly brave! Even as a young shepherd, he fought a lion and a bear! As a warrior, he won so many battles! I did not picture him as having fear. It is comforting, in a way, to realize that he said "when" I am afraid. That makes him relatable! I can learn from him.

Our very "way of life" is to trust in God. *The just shall live by faith* (Habakkuk 2:4). The book of Habakkuk revealed that the prophet did not deny his problems, nor did he treat them lightly; instead he found God sufficient in the midst of his troubles. We can do the same.

When I apply Hebrews 13:5-6 to my life, I've learned: God is with me, God is here for me, God has got this! No need to fear. Exodus 14:13-14 encourages me with the paraphrased message of: Don't be afraid, quiet your soul. God will fight this battle for you.

# I Am Beautiful ~ I Love Me!

*You formed my innermost being, shaping my delicate inside and my intricate outside, and wove them all together in my mother's womb (Psalm 139:13 TPT).*

*You and I are not mistakes or accidents! We were designed by a loving God who wanted us born and who welcomed us into this world! All the gifts and callings placed inside that tiny infant in the womb were planned by and put there by a Father whose love for us is huge! He created us to be a unique, one-of-a-kind blessing to our world.*

*Do you know Who You Are In Christ? Do you know What You Have in Christ? We are on the exciting journey of finding out what God says about us in His Word and then believing it is true for each one of us!*

# I Am Beautiful

How do you see yourself? How does God see you? Could it be that when God looks at you, He sees something different than what you see?

I don't think it is unusual for us to be in the dark about how God sees us. We seem to be limited to what we can see in the natural. It's only when we approach God, Who lives in the supernatural, that we can get a new perspective. Ask God - How do You see me? What do You see me doing in the future? Since He knows us and our potential, don't be surprised if He says some pretty awesome, mind-boggling things to you! All really good!

When God beholds us, He sees us through the lens of His love for us. When we look in a mirror, we can choose to use the lens of love as well. Knowing deep down that we are so totally and unconditionally loved makes us confidently look and feel beautiful!

God celebrated when each one of us were born! Who are we to not do the same? If our lives are precious to Him, then they should be precious to us as well. If He calls us beautiful, then we need to accept that and affirm it in our hearts. No more thinking we are "not good enough" in some area! We are linked to Jesus who is "Better than good!" When we do life with God, He makes us look good! He lets people think we are good looking, smart, spiritual and competent! All the while, we know that it is the Jesus in us that we're giving all the credit to! Jesus loves to live His life through us.

Don't compare yourself to someone you think is "more beautiful" than you in any way. That doesn't work! God only makes originals! He wants you to be the *Best You* there is! He put within you at birth all the qualities needed to be developed into a fabulous life! You have gifts and personality traits that are unique only to you!

God put us into the Beautiful One, Jesus, so He can't help but see us as beautiful too! We are entirely new! Old habits don't rule us, unless we let them rule. We've been born again into a new identity! That old "Adam life" part of us died with Christ on the cross. We were given a "Jesus life" to replace it, not just an upgrade of the old sinful nature. Our union with Jesus makes us Altogether Lovely, like He is!

*Father, thank You for calling each one of us "beautiful!" Thank You for seeing the best in us! You see all those beautiful things that You are responsible for birthing in us! We are so grateful for the grace You give to us!*

# I Am Valuable

You really are more valuable than you can ever imagine! Ask the One who created you in His image! When the Lord looks at you, He sees a precious person and no one knows you better than He does! Our identity is formed by how the Lord sees us, not how we see ourselves. Let's agree with Father and not focus on our own shortcomings.

*The kingdom of heaven is like a merchant seeking beautiful pearls, who, when he had found one pearl of great price, went and sold all that he had and bought it* (Matthew 13:45-46).

We are the beautiful pearl of great price that Jesus was looking for! Embrace the truth that every one of us is of great value to the Godhead! We were so valuable to the Father that He sent the Son of His Love to bear our sins on the Cross. Everything that kept us apart from a Holy God was done away with by our Savior's blood, shed for us. He "sold" all He had to get us!

It's because of love that Jesus was willing to pay the ultimate sacrifice to redeem us back to God. When we know and believe that He did that for each one of us individually (you and me!), we can't help but feel valued!

Perhaps you've tried other things to make yourself feel valuable. We humans do that. We think being a good person, marrying the right one, having a nice home and nice things, getting that great job and many other stipulations will help us to "count" in our own eyes and with people we know. It's after we get these things, THEN we will feel valued. No, we are valued NOW!

We can see ourselves like our Lord sees us: Chosen, Accepted, Loved with an everlasting love, Included, Never rejected, His beloved. Malachi 3:17 tells us that we belong to the Lord of Hosts and that He has made us His "jewels," His "special treasure." What if we used our own voice to speak out how the Lord sees us? "I am very special in the eyes of my Father." "I am a one-of-a-kind treasure to Him." "Father loves me with Big Loves just the way I am."

We have God's favor on our lives. (Psalm 5:12). He supplies all of our needs. (Philippians 4:13). He leads us with His eye upon us. (Psalm 32:8). He cares for us and we can tell Him everything. (1 Peter 5:7). We Are Valued!

*Father, You have given us so many reasons to know we are valuable! You are continually reminding us that we are very special to You just as we are! Help our hearts develop confidence in our own personal value.*

# *I Am Chosen*

In Season 2, Episode 2, of the popular tv series *The Chosen,* there is a scene where Phillip and Matthew are walking and talking. Matthew shared that he felt different from everyone else and he knew people hated him because he was a tax collector for the Romans. Phillip gave Matthew two truths to set him free. He said that people want to define us by our past. Once we meet Jesus, our past doesn't matter anymore. Now it's all about who we are in Him. Also, Matthew's significance came as a result of being chosen by Jesus.

Being chosen is something we can all say about ourselves! It was the heart of the Father to pursue each of us. He set us up! He worked in our heart and in our circumstances. We simply responded by asking Jesus to be our Lord.

Some of us have gotten used to being left out, even rejected. Childhood patterns have left their mark. It's hard to picture that we are truly chosen. It's then we can choose to speak words of truth from the Bible and drown out the negative voices from the past. Say out loud, "I am chosen! I am accepted by the only One who really matters! I'm important to Him!"

*He chose us in Him before the foundation of the world, that we should be holy and without blame before Him in love* (Ephesians 1:4). *He made us accepted in the Beloved* (Ephesians 1:6). We are chosen and accepted!

Some parents may say "that child was not planned, a mistake." You or I may have been a surprise to our parents, but not to God! Even before the world was formed, God knew us and He was calling and choosing us to be His children, each one with a special purpose to fulfill in this world.

Before there was an earth or sun or stars, God saw you and me! At that time, He separated us to Himself and enlisted us in His service. As much-loved sons and daughters of the King of the Universe, we bear the awesome privilege of walking in the high calling we have received by being chosen. His blessing, care and kindness inspire us to love and honor Him with our lives.

God has a unique purpose for each one of our lives. He put within us what it takes to perfectly fulfill that purpose. He chose us and designed us on the inside to fill a position that no one else can fill!

*Thank You Lord for seeing us, choosing us and calling us into Your service. We have no higher privilege! We believe You are a God who will bless and prosper us to do good things! Your Spirit enables us to serve You well.*

# *I Am Righteous*

Our righteousness is not about Doing, it is about Being. By faith we accept the gift of righteousness that Jesus bought for us. We cannot earn it. We will never deserve it, but we can own it and enjoy it.

*...Those who receive abundance of grace and the gift of righteousness will reign in life through the One, Jesus Christ* (Romans 5:17).

*For He made Him who knew no sin to be sin for us, that we might become the righteousness of God in Him* (2 Corinthians 5:21).

*For I will be merciful to their unrighteousness, and their sins and their lawless deeds I will remember no more* (Hebrews 8:12).

When we agree with God and see ourselves as righteous, it changes the way we think and act. For example, if you were wearing a white shirt or top, would you want to play in the mud? No! When we are conscious of our righteous identity in Christ, we would not want to become dirty with sin.

Even when we have just sinned, we can say, "I am the righteousness of God in Christ." Because of that belief, we are not defeated by our failings, but quickly repent and choose to do better with God's help. Condemnation doesn't rule us. We see ourselves as righteous, that's who we are! We are righteousness-conscious, not sin-conscious.

*...For our hearts have been sprinkled with blood to remove impurity, and we have been freed from an accusing conscience...* (Hebrews 10:22 TPT).

We are growing up into becoming truly righteous. The Holy Spirit was given to teach us how to think and act righteously. It is good to read the Word of God with a soft and pliable heart, willing to change. You and I ARE the righteousness of God in Christ. That's the Father's gift to us. And, we are BECOMING more righteous in our character as the Spirit helps us to be obedient to the teachings of the Bible.

*Father, thank You that no matter how many times I fail or how many mistakes I've made, I continue to wear the robe of righteousness that covers it all. (Isaiah 61:10). It is part of me now, a gift from God! When I miss the mark, I ask forgiveness, knowing this was an experience I can learn and grow from, making me more like Jesus, one lesson at a time. When thoughts come to remind me and bring shame, I strongly resist them! (Romans 8:1).*

# *I Am a Good Receiver!*

What if all God really wants is for us to come to Him, just as we are, and for us to be good receivers? I believe God wants to be a good giver! Daily. He's way more generous than we think. He doesn't dole out blessings sparingly!

To be a good receiver, we must start by being a good "truster!" When you trust another person, you're open with them. We can be open with God because we know He doesn't change. (Malachi 3:6). No matter what, He is faithful to His promises. He does what He says He will do! (Numbers 23:19).

*Pour out all your worries and stress upon him and leave them there, for he always tenderly cares for you* (1 Peter 5:7 TPT).

His tender care will strengthen us! Life affords plenty of opportunities to become frustrated and overwhelmed. It is then we must find out who God wants to be for us in each situation. What does He want to give us?

If we worry, He gives peace. When we're weak, He gives strength. When we don't know how to do something, He shows us how. When we are lonely, He comforts us. He has a positive for all of our negatives! These "positives" are found in the Word of God as promises that we <u>receive</u> by faith. Paul said the life he lived was by faith in the Son of God. (Galatians 2:20). God wants all of us to live by faith! (Habakkuk 2:4).

*I will instruct you and teach you in the way you should go, I will guide you with My eye* (Psalm 32:8). When we are taught, we learn truth. God teaches, we listen! God gives, we receive.

It's when we "go through stuff" that our priorities get sorted out. Being with Father to receive His guidance is what satisfies us. Talking to Him in prayer and listening to Him through reading His Word becomes a delightful habit.

God knows everything about us and everything about our circumstances. He give us the best advice! He has all wisdom! Faith to receive promises we need comes by hearing and hearing the Word. Then by hearing and hearing His promises some more! (Romans 10:17). Lots of "hearing the Word!"

*Father, thank You that in the good times and bad, You are there for us! We want to be good receivers! We will listen for Your instructions. We are encouraged by Your grace and power to help us in every situation. We receive Your wisdom and know You always show us the way that is best.*

## *I Know God As Father*

Do you know God personally as a Father? Do you want to? We already know for sure that He loves us and that He is very good to us. The Cross is the ultimate expression of the Father's love and goodness toward us.

*And because you are sons, God has sent forth the Spirit of His Son into your hearts, crying out, Abba, Father! Therefore you are no longer a slave but a son and if a son, then an heir of God through Christ* (Galatians 4:6-7).

We could have hidden barriers in our heart about having a personal relationship with the Father. Life sometimes does that to us. Some of us really have no clue about what a "good" father is like. It's hard to picture what God the Father is like because there was no example of a good father when growing up.

Friends talk about how their father made them feel special, was interested in their life, took them places, prayed for them, remembered what they liked, gave them good advice, told them they were loved, and on and on. Those who had no father or one that did none of those things cannot relate. They think, "Wow, that must have been nice! I wonder how it would feel to have a father like that." No worries. There is help!

God gave us an imagination for a reason! He wants us to use it! When you think of your heavenly Father, imagine He is just like the good father of your friends - only way better! Sometimes it helps to have an earthly picture.

*For the Holy Spirit makes God's fatherhood real to us as He whispers into our innermost being, You are God's beloved child* (Romans 8:16 TPT).

The Holy Spirit will show us the Father! Picture yourself freely sharing your heart completely with your heavenly Father. He hears it all, understands you and brings healing to your heart. He lets you know you are His very special, much-loved child who will always be welcome in His company.

*And when you pray, do not use vain repetitions as the heathen do, for they think that they will be heard for their many words. Therefore, do not be like them. For your Father knows the things you have need of before you ask Him* (Matthew 6:7-8). Isn't that good?! Let that truth sink in.

*Father, when Jesus prayed, "Our Father in heaven,"* (Matthew 6:9), *He was reminding us that God is OUR Father! Picture yourself as His favorite!*

# I Have a Purpose in Life

Don't ask your children what they want to do when they grow up, tell them to seek God and ask what He wants them to do. That's good advice for us grownups as well! For "seniors" reading this, God loves it when you decide to "finish well" by using your gifts (and wisdom) to serve where God leads.

Eric Liddell, the Olympic runner, made pleasing God his lifestyle and he would go anywhere he was led by his Lord, an easy place or a hard place. Eric lived his entire life completely surrendered to God.

Just like Eric, surrender is our starting place when we seek to live out our destiny. Each of us live under an "audience of One." We do what we do, not to show others how wonderful we are, but to simply fulfill the role which has been assigned to us by the Lord. Other people may be more charismatic or talented than you or I am. That doesn't concern us. We can rejoice for them. The grand works they are doing will not diminish what we are doing. God honors and rewards those who are simply obedient and faithful.

We were born with talents and abilities that are unique to us. Things that come easy for us. Things we enjoy doing. When we develop those abilities for the Lord's work, we shine for Him!

An example of differing abilities would be a Boss and Secretary. The Boss has the ability to see the big picture, to have a vision of how things should be. The Secretary knows how to help make those plans happen! She is not a visionary, but a detail-oriented person. The Boss doesn't concentrate on details and may not even care to! God made us to compliment each other. The body of Christ needs people with many different and unique talents to work together, just like the human body is made of different parts.

*Take My yoke upon you and learn from Me, for I am gentle and lowly in heart, and you will find rest for your souls. For My yoke is easy and My burden is light* (Matthew 11:29-30).

When you consider your purpose in life, do you see yourself yoked with Jesus, finding rest for your soul? Is Jesus is doing the heavy lifting and are you getting the easy and light part because you are yoked with Him?

*Father, help us to be increasingly surrendered to the plan you have for our lives. Our goal is to please the Father using the unique gifts and talents we were born with. We will keep in mind the Amazing Man we are yoked with!*

# I Have Faith

*"The just shall live by faith"* (Habakkuk 2:4). Living by faith gives us the best life! We can make living by faith the chief occupation of our lives! Knowing the promises of God and then receiving them by faith makes life enjoyable!

When we are fully persuaded that God loves us, it's easy for our hearts to have faith in Him. We can easily believe that all the promises in the Bible were put there just for us to take because we mean so much to Him.

Have you ever heard someone say, "let God love you?" God's part is that He has already decided to give and show love in abundance to each one of us! Now it's over to us to "learn how to be loved by Him." We practice accepting His love, not pushing it away, so there are no doubts left in our heart. When we first get out of bed, we can say over and over, "God loves me!" Yay!

Do we have even the slightest thought that God might lie to us? That He may not want to do for us what He has promised in His Word? Does He care enough to keep His Word? The story of the leper speaks to me.

*Now a leper came to Him, imploring Him, kneeling down to Him and saying to Him, If You are willing* (love me enough), *You can make me clean. Then Jesus, moved with compassion, stretched out*

*His hand and touched him, and said to him, I am willing;* (I love you enough), *be cleansed. As soon as He had spoken, immediately the leprosy left him, and he was cleansed* (Mark 1:40-42). Parenthesis added are my comments.

*Jesus Christ is the same yesterday, today, and forever* (Hebrews 13:8). What He did for the leper then, He will do for us today. We can place our faith in His love and His faithfulness toward us.

*For we walk by faith, not by sight* (2 Corinthians 5:7). The apostle Paul is telling the Corinthian church to not go by what they see with their eyes. Paul is also talking to us! Walking by faith and not by sight is something I have to pay attention to! Feelings can speak louder than God's promises! Read Habakkuk 2:2-3, *Though it tarries, wait for it; Because it will surely come.* I would add: Though it tarries, wait in faith for it. Keep on believing.

*Father, I thank You that You Love me 24/7! Thank You that my heart is established in Your love and goodness toward me. Because of that, I believe that You hear and answer my prayers! I have confident expectation that You are a good-to-me God, both able and willing to work wonders on my behalf.*

# *I Hear God*

It is important who we listen to and what we hear! *Man shall not live by bread alone, but by every <u>word</u> that proceeds from the mouth of God* (Matthew 4:4). Bread isn't enough. We must have a word from God!

God would be the best WHO we should listen to and His words would be the best WHAT we hear! Other voices are helpful, but we can always count on hearing the truth when reading our Bible. God speaks through His Word.

There are two Greek words used for our English "word" in the Bible: *logos* and r*hema. Logos* makes reference to the Bible in its entirety; *rhema* is a verse or verses that God uses to speak individually to His people.

In Matthew 4:4, quoted above, "word" is *logos.* We not only consume food, we consume God's entire Word to help our spirits grow. In Ephesians 6:17, "word" is *rhema,* which says the Word of God is our weapon of war!

*And take the helmet of salvation, and the Sword of the Spirit, which is the <u>Word</u> of God* (Ephesians 6:17). God is saying to use the Word as a sword!

We were designed to hear from our Father! Adam and Eve were created by God to walk and talk with Him. Jesus said, *My sheep hear My voice* (John

10:27). When we were born again, the Spirit was given to us. As we read the Bible, He illuminates a *rhema* word to us, just when we need it. He knows just what we need to hear and when we need to hear it!

Earthly fathers enjoy talking to their children. Our Heavenly Father desires to communicate with us, His kids. He likes to answer our questions too!

Help me Lord, to pay attention when I am reading my Bible, keeping alert for a word of correction, encouragement or direction. The Spirit of God helps us hear what our Father is saying. We don't live by bread alone! "Real Living" requires taking in, and benefitting from, what God is telling each one of us, our own *rhema* word to feed our soul. Rhema words are life-changing!

*Father, to be able to hear from You is a matchless treasure. You know us so well and love us so completely. Everything You say to us is to lift us up and make us better in every way. Your words are alive and powerful! (Hebrews 4:12). We do not take them for granted. Increase our desire to hear Your words, personal to us! May our hearts be guided by Your truth!*

# *I Focus On Christ in Me*

Have you invited Jesus to be your Lord and to live in your heart? If so, that's where He is right now! Even if we can't see Him or feel Him, He is there.

*Christ in you, the hope of Glory* (Colossians 1:27). *For in Him we live and move and have our being* (Acts 17:28).

*My old identity has been co-crucified with Messiah and no longer lives; for the nails of his cross crucified me with him. And now the essence of this new life is no longer mine, for the Anointed One lives his life through me - we live in union as one! My new life is empowered by the faith of the Son of God who loves me so much that he gave himself for me, and dispenses his life into mine!* (Galatians 2:20 TPT).

Jesus is in us and we are in Him! Our part is to receive that truth by faith and speak it out, celebrate it, depend on it and act as if it is true! Our identity will result in who our focus is on.

Is my focus on me or on the Person who is in me? If my focus is on me, I'm living by my performance; I'm trying to get it right! If my focus is on the Christ in me, I'm living in trust and rest. It boils down to trying or trusting.

Performance causes me to see my faults and failings. This results in guilt, shame and a negative image of myself. Thoughts of being a much-loved and treasured daughter fade away! I think the Lord is disappointed with me and has left me on my own to straighten up!

*I can do all things through Christ Who strengthens me* (Philippians 4:13). The emphasis is not so much on what I can achieve, but on how willing I am to allow Christ's sufficiency to flow through me. His strength is available to me in any circumstance. It's mostly about "through Christ," not "I can."

*Jesus Christ is the same yesterday, today, and forever* (Hebrews 13:8). That means that the same Jesus who strengthened you yesterday will be there for you today. The same Jesus that helped you before will be there in all your tomorrows to help you again. You can count on Him!

*Father, we have learned how to be "doers" and to not depend on anyone else! It's hard for us to "rest and receive!" Leaning on the grace of Jesus inside of us does not come naturally! Give us faith to stop "trying" and begin to continually "trust" in the Anointed One inside of us. HE is all we need!*

# *I Am Well Pleasing to God!*

When we were born again, we were put INTO CHRIST. Everything good in our lives right now is a result of what happened to us at our new birth. Now we have been given the choice to agree with, and to grow experientially into, what the Bible says about our union with Jesus.

When the Father says something about His Son (and we are united in our spirit with His Son), then what He says applies to both Jesus and to us.

*Behold! My Servant whom I uphold, My Elect (Chosen) One in whom My soul delights!* (Isaiah 42:1).

*And suddenly a voice came from heaven, saying, This is My beloved Son, in whom I am well pleased* (Matthew 3:17).

Jesus was Chosen and Beloved. We are chosen and beloved because we are in Him! The Father delights in Him. The Father delights in us! The Father is well pleased with Jesus. He is well pleased with us!

*Christ in you, the hope of glory* (Colossians 1:27). *You are complete in Him...* (Colossians 2:10). Jesus is IN US and we are IN HIM!

God the Father is a just Judge. Jesus was willing to take our place and pay the penalty for all of our sins, and that satisfied the justice of God. Now the Father freely forgives us, having judged Jesus on our behalf. God doesn't see a sin nature anymore, He killed it at the cross! Before Jesus, we were destined to die in our sins. *The soul that sins shall die* (Ezekiel 18:20). What amazing love Jesus has for us that He would die "as us" and "for us."

What do you see when you look at yourself? Do you picture your faults and failings? Do you see the things about yourself that are disappointing to you? Does that make you think God is also disappointed in you? He's not! You are His beloved in whom His soul delights! The sin barrier has been taken away!

When we read our Bible each day, we gradually and effortlessly, grow more in love with God and want to do life His way. Sin has lost its hold on us.

*Father, we need Your Spirit to help us understand our Position in Christ. Help us realize we no longer have a sin nature, simply a flesh habit that we can resist. When Jesus died, our sin nature died with Him. We were born again, born from above, now we have a "godly" nature! What a difference!*

# *I Love Myself!*

I am on a journey learning to love myself! I know, that sounds pretty arrogant, doesn't it? Like you're thinking right now, "Wow, her focus is just on herself, selfish to the max! Aren't we only supposed to love God with all our heart, soul, mind and strength?"

Let me explain. I mean, I'm learning to love myself the same way God loves me. He is quick to forgive. I want to be quick to repent and forgive myself as well. Since I am forgiven freely, I can forgive others freely. He is very patient with me. I want to practice being patient with myself...and with others. I can't give away what I don't have myself.

Question to myself: Have I been harsh, condemning and disappointed in myself - when God wasn't?

God loves us with *agape* love, the highest form of love. *Agape* believes the best about every person and does not ridicule or shame anyone. Even when Jesus was talking to the Pharisees in such a strong manner, His motive was to change their thinking to align with the message of God's love and grace instead of The Law. He cared for them enough to confront them with truth.

Sinners and kids loved to hang around Jesus! If He was harsh, rude and judgmental that would not happen. Jesus perfectly represented the Father.

*And to know the love of Christ, which passes knowledge, that you might be filled with all the fullness of God* (Ephesians 3:19).

Paul didn't tell the church in Ephesus to learn how to love Christ. He wanted them to really grasp the truth of the amazing love Jesus has for them. Paul knew they needed to experience divine love before they could give it away.

We all want to love God with all our heart. When we try to do that perfectly, we fail. We feel like we didn't love Him as much as He deserves.

_We love Him because He first loved us_ (1 John 4:19). We are loved by God, then we respond to that love and receive it into our hearts. We can now give His love away - back to Him, to our world - and also to ourselves!

*Father, how very privileged we are to be the object of Your amazing love. Help us to receive that healing love into the deepest part of our hearts. Give us the grace to love and value ourselves the same way You do.*

# *I Am Not Alone*

Besides believing we are loved by God, the belief that the Lord is with us is one of the most important beliefs we can have.

A precious and powerful promise that we can write our names on is: *My Presence will go with you, and I will give you rest* (Exodus 33:14).

Think of someone you greatly admire and respect, someone famous. Then imagine if that person wanted to be YOUR best friend! This person would love to hang out with you in your world and take you into their world.

How often have we viewed God as One who wants to spend the whole day with us? Do we have Him in the category of being "up there," not too far up there, but far enough so we can't see His face clearly? He is watching over us lovingly and showing us the plan He has for our lives. But, that is not the same as "doing daily life" down here in the real world that we live in.

Joseph was put in prison after being falsely accused by Potiphar's wife. GOD went to prison with Joseph! Anywhere you and I go, He wants to go there with us! It may be in a good situation, a really bad one, or something in between. It doesn't matter. God desires to extend mercy to us and give us His favor, even in the midst of our problems. He desires that we experience His Presence. The

Father wants to make our lives prosper, the same as He did for Joseph.

*The Lord was with Joseph and showed him mercy, and He gave him favor in the sight of the keeper of the prison. And the keeper of the prison committed to Joseph's hand all the prisoners...he did not look into anything that was under Joseph's authority, because the Lord was with him; and whatever he did, the Lord made it prosper* (Genesis 39:21-23).

Joseph learned that he couldn't look to people for encouragement or to fight his battles for him. There are many kinds of prisons. Are you in one right now? Is God in that prison with you? The God of Joseph answers with Yes!

*Father, I have chosen to believe that Your Presence will go with me, and You will give me rest. I welcome the experience of knowing Your Presence in new ways each day. Thank You that You care about me enough to want to be with me! And, because of Your Powerful Presence being with me each day, I can truly experience sweet rest in my soul. Whatever I do, You and You alone, will make it prosper. You, and You alone, will bring me through it all.*

# I Am an Original

*You formed my innermost being, shaping my delicate inside and my intricate outside, and wove them all together in my mother's womb. I thank You God for making me so mysteriously complex! Everything You do is marvelously breathtaking. It amazes me to think about it! How thoroughly You know me, Lord!* (Psalm 139:13-14 TPT).

You and I were created by the Best Artist, the Lord God! We are not a copy of anyone else, each one of us is an Amazing Original!

God carefully selected all the parts and colors of our bodies and made them perfect in our mother's womb. He chose the gifts and talents that would be put in seed-form inside of us. Even deciding on our personality type. He made us a "one-of-a-kind" for a reason. He had a purpose in mind for our lives way before we were born. A purpose that only we could fulfill.

We have an enemy who wants us to buy into the lie that we are not good enough. That God did not do a very good job when He created us. Satan gets us to focus on parts of our body or personality that we don't like and he makes us feel that we are deficient in those areas. He does what he can to keep us from believing we are perfectly and beautifully designed by God.

I cannot speak for men in regards to how they process self-worth. I'm a girl and I know from experience that we girls can be hard on ourselves. God wants us to embrace the unique and precious person he has made us to be. He wants us to affirm and appreciate that we are beautiful inside and out!

Have you ever looked at a woman who was not naturally pretty, but you thought she was beautiful because of the joy and love that bubbled out of her? How she cared about everyone around her and always had a smile? She brought the peace and presence of Jesus everywhere she went. She spoke encouraging words, never fault-finding words. She is a woman who is truly beautiful! She shines with the image of her Creator!

*Father, Thank You for designing me just the way I am! You gave me the color of my hair and eyes, and everything else about my unique body. Thank You for giving me the personality and the abilities You knew would fit me best. Everything I needed to accomplish Your purposes for my life was put in me, even in the womb. I was created in Your image and perfectly designed by You. I celebrate the beautiful person You've created me to be! I want to use the gifts and talents you've put inside of me to serve You!*

# *I Am Strong In Jesus*

When I married my husband, I gave up my last name and took on his name. The two of us became one unit. I got his bank account, the honor of sharing his successful career and numerous other benefits. I definitely got the best end of that deal!

The day that I became a Christian was a wonderful day! I gave Jesus all of me and I received all of Him in exchange. I *really* got the best part then! I became one with Jesus. Who He is, I am. What He has, I have. Wow.

Since I've been young, I've gotten pretty good at finishing the "I am ___" statements with something negative. I think some of the labels I've written on myself have been in permanent ink! It's not that I tried to do that or even thought too much about it, it just happened. Identity labels resulting from life and knowing my own faults and failings got buried in my heart.

Suppose you have a friend who struggles with not feeling good about herself. One day she said to you, "I am pathetic!" You were surprised by how transparent she was being with you. Your response was to say, "I know that you invited Jesus to be your Savior. You are in Him, which means you have been given His identity!" "Really?" she said. "Sure, you are not pathetic! Jesus is confident, therefore you are too since you are in Him! Just bury that old identity thinking and take on your true identity in Jesus!"

We gain a new identity when we are linked with the Godhead! It's not about being good enough, it's about resting in being "in Jesus" and Him in me.

Sin was taken care of at the cross. What can stumble me now are old mindsets. Freedom comes when I renew my mind with the Word. Jesus will help me change! It's about "who He is in me and for me." That's very different from being upset about the things I don't like about myself!

1 John 4:17, ...*As He is, so are we in this world.*

Ephesians 6:10, *I am strong in the Lord and the power of His might.*

Philippians 4:13, *I can do all things through Christ who strengthens me.*

*Father, thank You for giving us permission to think about ourselves like we really are - in Jesus! Negative identity labels in our hearts are being washed away, one at a time. All because You are trading our negative thoughts and habits for Your positive ones. Yay! We want to see ourselves like You do: strong, blessed and victorious in Jesus!*

# I Forgive Others and Myself

Ephesians 4:32 changed my life many years ago! As I meditated on each word, I knew God was speaking directly to me! *And be kind to one another, tenderhearted, forgiving one another, even as God in Christ forgave you.*

Becoming someone like Jesus, who forgave those who crucified Him, takes making a decision ahead of time. <u>I will forgive</u> because I have been forgiven by God. I realize there are traumatic experiences like abuse, abandonment, neglect and more that make forgiveness seem impossible. This is when it has to be two doing the forgiving; you and Jesus. Tuck your hurting heart into His huge heart of love and decide to let go of the wrong done to you. With His help, your heart will be healed and set free!

We are to forgive each other "even as" God in Christ forgives us. How does God forgive us? He doesn't bring up our offense ever! *Their sins and their lawless deeds I will remember no more* (Hebrews 10:17). God doesn't remember our faults and failings! I picture Him throwing them into a Sea of Forgetfulness where they are dissolved, completely gone! That's grace!

We forgive when someone has wronged us - and then we choose to forget the wrong done. We don't broadcast a person's sins. When we forgive, we set the person free! We set ourselves free too! Unforgiveness is a luxury that I cannot afford because it puts a distance between me and the Father. I don't want that. I'm sure you don't either.

Some find it is easier to forgive someone else than to forgive themselves. All of us have regrets. We also have an accuser who brings to mind things in our past. His goal is to make us feel guilty and ashamed, not worthy of any of God's blessings. We can say, "I've repented and been forgiven by the blood of Jesus, so I reject all condemnation! I throw this thought into the Sea of Forgetfulness!" We may have to do that many times a day at first!

Forgiving ourselves is a process. First, we have to recognize that negative thoughts are not coming from ourself, they are coming from the enemy. At the cross you and I were forgiven for everything! Nothing was too big and nothing too small, Jesus paid it all and gave forgiveness to us as a gift.

*Father, we need Your grace to help us forgive others and grace to forgive ourselves. Does it make You sad when You have forgiven us, but we choose not to forgive ourselves? The devil is the winner then. No! Not happening!*

*Jesus is the winner and always will be! And, He makes us winners too!*

# I Have a Destiny

As the apostle Paul said goodbye to the elders he had ministered to and with for the past three years in Ephesus, he shared his heart with them. He told them the Holy Spirit was sending him to Jerusalem where chains and afflictions awaited him.

*But whether I live or die is not important, for I don't esteem my life as indispensable. It's more important for me to fulfill my destiny and to finish the ministry my Lord Jesus has assigned to me...* (Acts 20:24 TPT).

Paul is basically saying that his life did not have to be precious in his own sight because it was precious in the eyes of his Lord Jesus and that was enough for him. He knew Jesus had a destiny and an assignment for him.

Paul is also letting us know that our lives count! That each one of us has been given an assignment from the Lord, a destiny. It's our part to talk to the Lord about what He has in mind for us. Let's not be surprised if what we hear from Him is way bigger than we would come up with! Of course, it has to be that way so we always depend on Him to accomplish it though us.

Paul's starting point was the Lordship of Jesus in his life. That should be our starting point as well. If we continue to be our own "lord," to make decisions on our own, we will miss the very best that life holds for us. There's nothing better than seeing Jesus do beautiful things in us, to us and through us. Jesus is the most beautiful Person ever! Let's let Him live His beautiful life through us! Then say goodbye to "boring!"

Don't accept the lie that you are not qualified. We can disqualify ourselves when God has not. God is the One who qualifies us! We are all called! If you have made Jesus your Savior and Lord, you are now a part of the "set apart" ones to do His will.

Which statement is true: "I can" or "I can't?" They are both true, depending on what you choose to believe. The "I can" people are trusting in God's promises and His strength. The "I can't" people only see their limitations and fears. The children of Israel saw giants while Caleb and Joshua saw a Big God! You and I have that same Big God!

*Father, help us to be "I can" people, because we are servants of the "nothing is impossible God!" We are joined to the One who will qualify us for anything He asks us to do. Lord, we are available, show us our destiny!*

# I Am Renewing My Mind

*And do not be conformed to this world, but be transformed by the renewing of your mind, that you may prove what is that good and acceptable and perfect will of God* (Romans 12:2).

Being conformed to this world means we allow ourselves to be influenced by and to accept the pattern of this age, whose god is the devil. We inwardly and outwardly will reflect the world's ways.

On the contrary, we are to be transformed (changed) by the renewal of our minds. How do we renew our minds? By reading and pondering the Word of God. God's Word is truth that soaks into our heart, giving us new attitudes and new thought patterns. We gain the ways of the Kingdom of God.

We can look back and see how the Lord has led us to do the right things because we have kept our focus on the Word of God. We do the right things with the right attitudes! Positive emotions like Joy and Peace come from opening up the Scriptures. Right up until we die, we will still be transformed, made into the likeness of Jesus, by the renewing of our minds.

When we make Bible reading a priority, the Holy Spirit radically transforms the way we think. We turn our backs to the ways of the world. It doesn't satisfy us anymore. We become surrendered to the ways of God and *present our bodies a living sacrifice, holy, acceptable to God* (Romans 12:1).

In John 17, Jesus prays for all of us: *They are not of this world, just as I am not of this world* (v16). *Sanctify them* (set them apart) *by Your truth. Your Word is truth* (v17). His Word is Spirit and life. (John 6:63).

Hebrews 4:12 begins by saying, *The Word of God is living and powerful.* God's Word has the potential of working powerfully in our lives! We must activate it by believing it, speaking it and acting as if it is true!

I've heard there are over 7,000 promises in the Bible. What would happen if we put our name on the ones that matched our situation? Would we see the power of God meet our needs? Sure! What verses are you standing on?

*Father, we believe Your Word and we see our situations change! God confirms His Word - "I have spoken it, I shall bring it to pass"* (Isaiah 46:11). *We consider God to be alive and relevant in our lives. We choose to believe His Word is truth, therefore we say "amen" to His promises!*

# I Am Priceless

We were actually "purchased" with the precious blood of Jesus. Therefore, in God's eyes, we are "priceless." Because He has chosen to call us priceless doesn't give us a reason to be proud. On the contrary, it humbles us to know He has lifted us to such a position in His sight. We are eternally grateful.

None of us are worthy of the kindness of God. We don't deserve any of it. We don't deserve His mercies, but they are new every morning. I know that I am unworthy of His faithfulness toward me over the years. For us to be "unworthy" does not mean we are "worthless." God considers us worth the very best that there is, and ever was, the life-blood of His Beloved Son.

When we begin to see ourselves as priceless, we can see others as priceless as well. It will change the way we look at them and treat them. We will value people with the same standard as God values them. Jesus gave His life for all of us, saint and sinner alike. We receive grace and then give it away!

We choose daily whether to think positively or negatively about ourselves. It's good to say things like: "I am Beautiful, I am Valuable and I have a Purpose in Life." Also, quoting Jeremiah 29:11 over ourselves will assure us that God does have a purpose and a plan for our lives! These truths and others from the Bible will help to keep our thinking positive.

What we think and believe has a direct effect on our emotions. When you are feeling really negative, ask yourself - What am I saying to myself right now? Does it line up with what God says about me in His Word? Are my thoughts agreeing with truth or lies? A lie will hold us captive, but the truth will set us free! We ARE Beautiful, Valuable and we do have a Purpose!

Do you know anyone who has been so beaten down by life that they think they are worthless? Things have not worked out well for them and they feel it is most likely all their fault. Sure, mistakes have been made and bad decisions brought unpleasant consequences. However, there is no point so low that Jesus is not there to pick that weary one up and walk with them on a good path to success. When we get to heaven, we will hear stories about ones who were rescued and restored by the love and power of Jesus.

*Father, may each one of us keep our hearts open to help the "down and out" in some way. Every soul is priceless! "He that wins souls is wise" (Proverbs 11:30). We can treat others how we want to be treated. Father, please build our faith and give us Your compassion to help a weaker brother or sister.*

# I Have Peace

How do we get a sense of peace? Can we buy it? Like go on a cruise or to the beaches of Hawaii to "get peaceful?" Can we wish for it, like hoping for a raise at work? What do you do to obtain that illusive feeling of peacefulness?

What is peace? How would you describe it? To me, it's a feeling of safety and comfort. We need peace the most when we are worried and fearful or when we are unsure, not knowing what to do.

We can have 100 lbs of pressure coming at us from the outside, but if we have 101 lbs of peace on the inside, we will not be moved.

How do I gain peace? And keep it when negative things hit me? We receive it as a gift from Jesus. He said, *Peace I leave with you, My peace I give to you, not as the world gives do I give to you. Let not your heart be troubled, neither let it be afraid* (John 14:27). Focus on Jesus and receive His supernatural kind of peace. Jesus, thank You for Your peace. We take it!

Jesus reminds us to *let not your heart be troubled.* The "let not" is our part. We turn our eyes away from our problem, laying it all down at His feet and leaving it there. Jesus loves us! We can trust Him with anything.

"He is able, He is willing, to make all things become new. We walk by faith and not by sight, to prove our Savior true." This is part of little poem I wrote in a difficult time in my life. I endured that season carried along by God's sweet peace. The peace of God is powerful!

*You will keep him in perfect peace, whose mind is stayed on You, because he trusts in You* (Isaiah 26:3). "Perfect peace" sounds good to me; you too?

Exodus 14:14 tells us that the Lord will fight our battles for us! We can hold our peace (be quiet). Exodus 15:2 says, *The Lord is my strength and song and has become my salvation* (saves me from any difficulty!).

*For He Himself has said, I will never leave you nor forsake you. So we may boldly say: The Lord is my helper; I will not fear* (Hebrews 13:5-6).

*Father, thank You for the gift of Jesus, the Prince of Peace, to live inside of us! Thank You for making Your sweet and powerful peace available to us!*

# I Am Made in His Image

*God created man in His own image; in the image of God He created him; male and female He created them* (Genesis 1:27).

We are like God in that we can reason, make moral decisions and we have a conscience. We have a personality, intellect and more. We are copies of Him!

When Adam was created, God breathed into him a dual nature. His body had access to the natural realm with natural senses to see, hear, etc. What if the spirit part of him had those same senses which gave him access into the supernatural realm of God? Adam and his wife Eve enjoyed daily encounters with God. Could they see His glory?

If so, all of that changed when they disobeyed God and ate the forbidden fruit. The spirit part of them died, just as God said it would. They believed the lies of the serpent and chose sin over having fellowship with their Maker.

Everyone from Adam onwards was born missing the spirit part of man. Only the natural part, the "soul" part, was left.

Wait! God had a plan to make it possible for man to have the spirit part restored! Jesus explained to Nicodemus that when we ask Christ to be the Lord of our life, we are born again. The birth of the Spirit of God within us restores us back to the original creation where we possess both a natural and a spiritual nature.

We can get as closely knit to the Father's heart as we want to be. We're no longer separated from God because of sin, but set free to walk and talk with the Creator of the Universe. All because of the grace and mercy of God expressed at the cross.

The door to God's heart is always open to us. He invites us into His realm. *When You said, Seek My face, my heart said to You, Your face, Lord, I will seek* (Psalm 27:8). David found such pleasure being in God's company.

*Draw near to God and He will draw near to you* (James 4:8). We are encouraged to pursue a close relationship with the Father.

*Father, You call us near ~ we draw near. Either way we end up in the secret place of Your sweet Presence. This is where revelation comes, heart-healing happens and where we are strengthened and refreshed.*

# *I Am a Work in Progress!*

Jesus and Martha were good friends. In Luke 10:38-42 we read of a visit Jesus made to her home. Knowing that they would all be hungry soon, Martha got busy in the kitchen making some of her best recipes. All the while, her sister Mary was no help at all, which added to her frustration.

Picture this scene in your mind. What do you think motivated Martha to go to all that trouble in the kitchen? Was it simply her duty, as she was possibly the oldest sibling? Verse 38 says that *Martha welcomed Him into her house.* Do you think that she thought if she put on a splendid feast that Jesus would appreciate her more, maybe honor her with a compliment?

What about us in the here and now? What is our motivation for serving Him? Simple obedience to God without thought of recognition? Or do we want to be recognized? Do we feel by doing more we will be appreciated more?

It wasn't that Martha was preparing a meal, it was that she was making the meal unnecessarily a big deal! She became *worried and troubled about many things* when she could have opened cans of soup. (I know there were no cans of soup in those days, but you get the picture of something "relatively" easy.) She could have cut big chunks of bread, knowing Jesus and the guys would have been fine with soup and bread! Jesus wanted to "feed Martha" with words of truth. Her soul was important to Him.

In Revelation 2, Jesus spoke to the church at Ephesus. He complimented them for their hard work and perseverance and many other things. However, Jesus said they had abandoned the love they had for Him in the beginning. For that reason alone, Jesus said He would remove their lamp stand, their church, if they did not repent. Jesus is letting us know His priorities.

Jesus came to offer Martha a relationship of close fellowship with Him. That comes before works of service. It was all about her learning the <u>best way</u> to express her love for her Master. Aren't we all learning, just like Martha? I am definitely learning! I am a work in progress. Help me listen and love!

*Father, help us to listen to that still small voice that tells us what to do in each situation. If Jesus says soup and bread, then that's what it is! The ways of Jesus are always best. "Be still and know that He is God" (Psalm 46:10). Father, help us to start out each day with words of adoration, praise and thanksgiving to our Matchless Lord Jesus. Before we focus on the work He has given us to do, let's let Him know that HE Alone is the One we Love!*

# *I Lean On Jesus*

The heart of our Christian life and experience is demonstrated by the contrast between John's point of view and Peter's point of view at The Last Supper. Jesus announced that one of them would betray Him. None of the twelve had a clue as to who would do such a thing!

*The disciple that Jesus dearly loved was at the right of Him at the table and was leaning his head on Jesus* (John 13:23 TPT).

Notice that John was leaning his head on Jesus. Our head is where we think. We figure things out and come to conclusions. Leaning indicates that John is resting in Jesus, confident of His love. John's life was liberated by realizing how special he was to Jesus. You and I can choose to "Rest in Being Loved." That is a truth to speak out and claim for ourselves!

Mention is made of where John was sitting - "at the right of Him at the table." This could be a figure of speech for "the place of honor." (Jesus sat down at the right hand of God. (Mark 16:19). The disciple John represents all of us! Ephesians 2:6 says, *God has made us sit together in the heavenly places in Christ Jesus.*

Later in the conversation, Jesus told His disciples that He was leaving and they would not follow at that time, but would follow Him later. Peter said,

*Why can I not follow You now? I will lay down my life for Your sake* (John 13:37). Life without Jesus was not happening! Peter was a born leader, a "take charge" man. He wanted to "fix" this situation. (Do we do that?)

John enjoyed "<u>receiving</u> love from Jesus." Peter said, "<u>I will</u> even die for You, I love You so much!" Peter thought he was strong, well able to handle any adversity. Does he remind you of a crowing rooster, strutting in pride?

Peter ran away, sobbing. He realized that strength did not originate in him. The old way was for man to love God with all his heart. The new way is to Live Loved by God first, then we have what it takes to love Him back.

John took strength from knowing he was loved, and ended up being the disciple to stand close to the cross. Where were the other disciples?

*Father, Peter, like Martha, "grew up in public!" And, oh my, how he grew up! Fabulous what You did with him - 3,000 saved at Pentecost, Leader of the Apostles and the early church! Hey, even his shadow was powerful!*

# *I Am Beautiful References*

### p50-51   I Am Chosen

Dallas Jenkins, Creator/Director of the tv series The Chosen, Season Two, Episode Two. Angel Studios, Provo, UT

### p58-59   I Have a Purpose in Life

*Eric Liddell: Champion of Conviction DVD* (Worcester, PA, Christian History Institute, Distributed by Vision Studio). Joyce Stranks, her video testimony of being with Eric Liddell when he died. She said Eric's last word was surrender.

### p62-63   I Hear God

Dick Mills, *Word Wealth,* Definition of "word," *Spirit Filled Life Bible, NKJV, Jack W. Hayford, General Editor* (Nashville: Thomas Nelson, 1991), 1408.

# 1 Corinthians 13:4-8
## ~ Loving Others

*The best way to be refreshed in our own heart is to ponder how much God loves us. The best way to help another person is to find ways to love and serve them unconditionally, no reward expected. Love softens hearts. Love changes things! And Love Heals!*

*This section is about how to be a channel for the powerful love of God to flow through our lives. We represent the Godhead! We are re-presenting Jesus and the Father to people. We present their nature and character through our attitude and actions. Help us Father, to re-present You well!*

*Each truth described in verses 4 through 8 is well worth pondering deeply. When we give ourselves to be fully committed to Christ and His cause, we must own and practice these truths about how Love behaves. By showing patience, kindness and the rest, we are winsome representatives of Christ for the world to see and to want what we have!*

# 1 Cor 13:4 <u>Love suffers long,</u> having patience with imperfect people.

**From God's point of view:** You imagine that because you are "imperfect" that I lose patience with you. That is not true. I am very patient with you because that is what Love does. I have put you into My Son Jesus, the Perfect One. Jesus will help you become more like Himself as you just live day by day with Him. Stop trying to "be perfect!" Enjoy being in Christ.

**From my point of view:** Every once in a while, I encounter people who are "not completely perfect!" I noticed the ones that try my patience the most are the ones who have the same imperfections that I have!

My heavenly Father is aways kind-hearted and patient toward me. I am so thankful for Him! He helps me learn from my mistakes and gives me the grace to do better the next time. Jesus did not judge anyone He met and He doesn't judge me. Therefore, I must not judge others. When do I appreciate God's patience the most? When I am disappointed in myself. Then, Father lets me know He is still on my side, still has great plans for my life and still thinks the best of me! I must remind myself that God wants me to be patient with myself too! I am a work in progress!

Patience describes a person who has the opportunity to take revenge but instead chooses to use restraint. Patience is a quality of God's kind of love that wants the highest and best for all.

**Definition of words:**

Suffers - allows, puts up with, is kind-hearted toward

Patience - reacts kindly, holds steady, cancels negative emotions

Imperfect - less than the best quality, flawed, rejected, inferior

**A Decision of My Heart:**

*Dear Father, as an act of my will, I decide that from now on, with Your help, I will choose to be aware that You are with me during those times when I am tempted to have a bad attitude. That is when I sense Your love and patience with me. That consciousness will allow me to also be patient with an irritating person! What I have been given, I can also freely give away. When I lean on You in me, Your patience just flows out naturally!*

# 1 Cor 13:4 *Love is kind,*
## *active in doing good.*

**From God's point of view:** God is forever kind to us. He is always the same and will never change. His kindness to us is exemplified by the many good things He does for us. Every day we can look back on His kindnesses. Psalm 119:68 tells us that God is good and He does good! And, He assures us that His goodness will follow us all the days of our lives! (Psalm 23:6).

**From my point of view:** Kindness is the ability to act for the welfare of those taxing our patience. Perhaps we have social relationships that require us to walk in a spirit of love and warmth when we may not feel like expressing those things at all! That's when we must depend on our "Forever Kind God" to love through us. Kindness is Love in Action! The more we are convinced that we are loved, the more we can pass that love to others by treating them kindly. Like God treats us!

*"Command those who are rich in this present age not to be haughty, nor to trust in uncertain riches but in the living God, who gives us richly all things to enjoy. Let them do good, that they may be rich in good works, ready to give, willing to share"* (1 Timothy 6:17-18).

**Definition of words:**

Kind - gentleness in dealing with others, sweetness of disposition

Active - movement, action, doing something

Doing Good - wanting the best for others, helping them to succeed

**A Decision of My Heart:**

*Dear Father, as an act of my will, I decide that from now on, with Your help, I won't look at the faults of others. I will concentrate on how I can be used by You to help people receive Your Love and Kindness. I can demonstrate by good deeds and kindness what You are really like.*

*Thank You for showing me that loving people through my life is Your heart and priority. Kindness and goodness are part of Who You are and what You want everyone to experience. Our lives are not all about getting noticed or even thanked. Our lives are all about sharing with others what we have received from God. We can show God's love by doing random acts of kindness and performing thoughtful good deeds.*

# 1 Cor 13:4 <u>Love does not envy;</u> it cheers for others!

**From God's point of view:** God is our biggest Cheerleader! He plans for and wants the best for each one of us. He can see potential in us that even we cannot see. God desires that we get to know and have fellowship with people who love the Lord. It doesn't matter about ages or stages of growth, it simply matters about the love that covers all relationships.

## Since Love is non-possessive and non-competitive, it actually wants other people to get ahead.

**From my point of view:** It is easy to look at other believers and think that they are like "heroes" and I am so far from that! Or, it could also be the other way around. It does not pay to compare; it always leads us into the trap of either thinking we are better than, or worse than, others. The key is to not want to be someone else! We can appreciate the gifts that others have, but it is also important to acknowledge, appreciate and develop the gifts that we ourselves have. We don't compete with others, nor do we envy them, we compliment them and want to see them succeed!

**Definition of words:**

Envy - wanting to be or to have what someone else is or has

Non-Possessive - every good thing we have is a Gift from God

Non-Competitive - we don't always have to win or be the best

**A Decision of My Heart:**

*Dear Father, as an act of my will, I decide that from now on, with Your help, I will keep in mind that my strengths and abilities are not what I earned, but what I was given by God and His Grace. I choose not to flaunt those gifts, but neither to hide them. I put them under the control of the Lord to be used for the benefit of others. God made us to bless one another! Since it was our extremely wise Creator God who chose which gifts would fit me the best, who am I to want someone else's talents or abilities?*

*I consider it a benefit to have a variety of godly voices speaking into my life. I choose not to envy what they have, but to be thankful for the unique way they have blessed me, helping me to grow in the Lord.*

# 1 Cor 13:4 <u>Love does not parade itself.</u> Love has a self-effacing quality; it is not ostentatious.

**From God's point of view:** The Bible says, For God SO LOVED the world that HE GAVE us Jesus. It's God's nature to love and to give. He wants us to have that same nature. When our focus is on Him and not on ourselves, we change from the inside out and become more like Him. We become more loving and giving, not caring so much on "what people think!"

**From my point of view:** A "self-effacing" person does not call attention to himself or herself. No need for boasting in what we have done. No need for us to try to make ourselves "look good" to others! No need to make an impression on anyone! That just turns out to be "parading ourself!" Love doesn't do that.

We are outrageously loved by the One Who Created Everything, and that helps us to keep things in perspective. God is in charge of our reputation! What matters is we know that the Father smiles on us every day.

**Definition of words:**

Parade itself - wanting people to see and appreciate me

Self-effacing - not putting oneself or one's actions in the limelight

Ostentatious - attempting to impress others

**A Decision of My Heart:**

*Dear Father, as an act of my will, I decide that from now on, with Your help, I will put my focus on You, where it belongs. I will thank You for opportunities to serve You without looking for accolades. I possess dignity simply because I am Your child, part of Your Eternal Family!*

*Show me times when any arrogance shows up in my attitude so that I can repent. I want to represent Your Love well. Times when I feel the need to "look better" or "be smarter" just may mean I am revealing some hidden insecurity in myself. I choose contentment over insecurity, knowing that I am secure in Your amazing Love and Care for my life.*

*It takes humility to make myself and my actions inconspicuous. Please work that humility in me. Help me, Father, to not attract notice or try to impress others. There is only One Impressive One and His Name is Jesus!*

# 1 Cor 13:4 <u>Love is not puffed up,</u> treating others arrogantly.

**From God's point of view:** God is never high-handed with us, acting as a demanding tyrant. Even when He is correcting us, He does it in gentleness, letting us know that He will help us to change. Yes, He is firm with us, letting us know that to choose His ways mean we are choosing the best for ourselves. He never pushes us into a corner with rebukes, but always provides a better way to think and live.

**From my point of view:** The "I'm right and you're wrong, end of story" approach doesn't turn out very well! It seems there is always another side to every story. It pays to be open-minded enough to be willing to listen first before rushing to judgment.

Discussing an issue with God in prayer is essential. Let Him give me advice and counsel before I make matters worse with a "know-it-all" attitude. I have come to think that Humility surely can be called one of the best virtues we can have! When we humble ourselves, God will lift us up and give us grace. (James 4:6,10). Titus 3:2 says, *"Speak evil of no one, be peaceable, gentle, showing all humility to all men."* Jesus is our example. He humbled Himself and became obedient, even to death on the cross. (Philippians 2:8).

## Definition of words:

Puffed Up - Thinking more highly of myself than I should

Arrogantly - Looking down on others, speaking down to others

## A Decision of My Heart:

*Dear Father, as an act of my will, I decide that from now on, with Your help, I will take the winning approach of humility. That means that I will listen to all sides of an issue before I come to a conclusion. It means that I will honor someone else's opinion. It means that I won't gossip about anyone.*

*In no way do I want to discredit someone else's reputation or diminish their dignity. I refuse to make myself look good while making someone else look bad. I will not side with the "accuser of the brethren."*

*I will choose not to prefer one person over another because of rank or status. All people are precious because they are made in God's image, not because they hold a high position somewhere. Help me, Lord, to see beyond the outward image of a person and be able to see their heart.*

# 1 Cor 13:5 <u>Love does not behave rudely,</u> but displays good manners and courtesy.

**From God's point of view:** It would not occur to God to speak to us the same way we sometimes speak to one another! Even when He is letting us know we need a course correction in our attitude or actions, He is kind. He does not push us into a corner and berate us! That would be the devil's way. God always offers His help for us to change and also shows us a better path to take. Responding positively to His correction means we are getting an upgrade in life in every way!

**From my point of view:** When I choose to walk in love, it involves being careful about how I present myself to others. I can come across as rough or harsh or I can show a kind spirit. It helps to remind myself of what the apostle Paul spoke to the Ephesian church: *"And never let ugly or hateful words come from your mouth, but instead let your words become beautiful gifts that encourage others; do this by speaking words of grace to help them"* (Ephesians 4:29 TPT). Peter tells believers to have these attitudes: *"Finally, all of you be of one mind, having compassion for one another; love as brothers, be tender hearted, be courteous, not returning evil for evil or reviling for reviling, but on the contrary blessing, knowing that you were called to this, that you may inherit a blessing"* (1 Peter 3:8-9).

**Definition of words:**

Rudely- impolite, especially in a deliberate way

Good Manners - displaying kindness and graciousness

Courtesy - respectful, considerate of others

**A Decision of My Heart:**

*Dear Father, as an act of my will, I decide that from now on, with Your help, I will take Your Word as my Guide when it comes to interacting with people. It doesn't take long for a person to read my heart. I show it in my smile and the way I look directly into their eyes, giving them my full attention. That makes them feel important to me. Help me to speak with kindness and always for their benefit. I want the person in front of me to feel they are loved by God and by me!*

## 1 Cor 13:5 <u>Love does not seek its own,</u> insisting on its own rights.

**From God's point of view:** God has made a way for us to Live in Christ through the cross and the resurrection. When we are born again, the Bible says that Jesus comes to make His residence inside of our hearts, our innermost being. Actually, He comes not just to keep us company, He comes to sit on the throne of our hearts. To be King and Lord of our lives.

**From my point of view:** When I said "Yes" to God's invitation to be a part of His family, I was actually saying "Yes" to a surrendered life. At the time, I was very happy to hand over my messed-up life to a higher power! Over the years of walking with the Father, I've experienced how His Love can heal and restore my heart. He is the Source of all the good things that have come my way and I am so thankful. When I received Christ, I gave up "my rights!" No more seeking my own way. Now I am trusting in His way for me. It always turns out the best that way!

I've learned over the years that "ministry" is not having my name on the door of an office or on a badge of authority. Ministry is first to the Lord in adoration and praise. Then it is being conscious of Him throughout the day. Ministry is what you and I do or say when we feel prompted by the Lord.

Everything He does is loving, kind and helpful. We are His hands and feet to express those things!

## Definition of words:

Seek its own - try to obtain for self

Its own rights - wanting authority, benefits and priority

## A Decision of My Heart:

*Dear Father, as an act of my will, I decide that from now on, with Your help, I will not live my life based on my own reasoning and inclination! Help me not to be in a hurry about making important decisions. Remind me how vital it is to get Your guidance and wisdom. Thank You that You are a Good Father and you know all of my needs. Thank You for Your care for me, that I don't have to try to obtain anything for myself. I simply cast my cares on You. You will provide everything I need according to Your riches in glory. Instead of "insisting on my own rights," I lay down my rights at the foot of the cross and I simply trust in You.*

# 1 Cor 13:5 <u>Love is not provoked;</u> it is not irritable or touchy, but is graceful under pressure.

**From God's point of view:** We sometimes get the idea that God is a bit disappointed in us and therefore He keeps His distance from us. But, those are lies that have gotten into our head! He is not that way at all. How do we know what the Father is really like? We can look at Jesus. "He came, not to judge us, but to set us free!" (John 12:47) Jesus performed countless deliverances and healings and for people who weren't perfect! He didn't say - "all of you who have issues in your life, go and get holy and then come back and I will heal you!" He knew we were not able to do that. "He saw our frame, that we were dust and He had pity on us." (Psalm 103:13-14) God's Love for us is expressed in showing grace to us.

**From my point of view:** My shortcomings don't call forth feelings of anger or exasperation from Jesus or the Father. We do give away what we have received, and that would be lots of grace! When I'm under pressure is the time when it is easier to be irritable or touchy. That's when I must quiet myself and depend on the Enabler, the Lord who lives within me, to help me respond with grace.

The word "grace" means "unmerited favor," "undeserved blessing," and "a free gift." A characteristic of Love is being full of grace, even under pressure.

## Definition of words:

Provoked - stir up feelings, desires, activity

Irritable - easily annoyed, impatient

Graceful - full of grace, treating others better than they deserve

## A Decision of My Heart:

*Dear Father, as an act of my will, I decide that from now on, with Your help, I will trust You to keep me from becoming impatient. Especially, please guard my lips from speaking unkind words. Put a check in my spirit when I am getting annoyed or becoming offended. Quiet my soul with Your peace. Teach me how to be a "grace giver!" Help me treat people the way I would like to be treated.*

*"A soft answer turns away wrath"* (Proverbs 15:1).

## 1 Cor 13:5 <u>Love thinks no evil;</u> *it does not keep an account of wrongs done to it; instead it erases resentments.*

**From God's point of view:** Of course, God hates evil. For the simple reason it is destructive. He gave us the Ten Commandments like signs in a mine field. DANGER! Don't walk there! It will not go well with you! All the evil of the whole of mankind was laid upon Jesus on the cross. He buried it when He died. The Father looks at everyone now without condemnation, not wanting anyone to perish.

**From my point of view:** *"Love covers all sins"* (Proverbs 10:12). Next to that verse I have written in my Bible: "Don't sweat the small stuff! Let love for God and others be my aim!" The "small stuff" describes irritations, offenses and rude people that seem to find their way across our path! When they come, it gives us a perfect opportunity to let it go, like water off a duck's back! Talk to my hurt feelings and say - we're just going to love God and others. That's it. (Feelings are fed by what we think and say.)

*"Do not be overcome by evil, but overcome evil with good"* (Romans 12:21). This is called "moving in the opposite spirit." When a person does their best to hurt you in some way - and you respond by treating them kindly, it shakes them! In that moment you are acting with God's Supernatural

Love! *"Vengeance is Mine, I will repay, says the Lord"* (Romans 12:19).

## Definition of words:

Thinks no evil - No thoughts of revenge or hatred toward someone

Keep an account - a bookkeeping term, adding up the offenses

Resentments - a heart hardened by offenses

## A Decision of My Heart:

*Dear Father, as an act of my will, I decide that from now on, with Your help, I will be quick to ask for Divine Help so that any resentment, even a small one, won't be like a loop tape in my mind. I want my first reaction to be - "I hardly even notice when others do me wrong." Father, I can only do that when You help me let go of offenses. Left to myself, I can get offended quite easily! That leads to strained relationships with people and with You. I know You will bless me as I refuse to keep a record of anyone's wrongs.*

# 1 Cor 13:6 <u>Love does not rejoice in iniquity,</u> finding satisfaction in the shortcomings of others and spreading an evil report.

**From God's point of view:** How can God rejoice in iniquity when He doesn't even think about it?! He is not sin-conscious. Hebrews 10:12 says, *"But this Man, after He had offered one sacrifice for sins forever, sat down at the right hand of God."* And, in verse 14 - *"For by one offering He has perfected forever those who are being sanctified, (set apart)."* Our spirit has been made alive (perfected forever) by the blood of Christ. What an amazing trade happened on the cross! God took our sin and punished Jesus for it. Then He took the righteousness of Christ and gave it to us as a gift! Now we deal with the desires of our flesh. Jesus comes alongside to aid us in living more from our spirit, less from our flesh. No judgment, just helping us!

**From my point of view:** Because of what happened at the cross, I can say with confidence that I don't have to be conscious of my sins or anyone else's sins or shortcomings. I welcome God's words of correction. They are always given with love and I know are for my benefit. I reject feelings of guilt and condemnation. And, I refuse to find satisfaction when others don't live up to "my standard!" If that person pleases God, then they please me. If that person does not please God, then God can change them! My part is to always support, love and pray for others, not to fix them or set them straight! That would be God's part and He does His part so well!

## Definition of words:

Rejoice in iniquity - laughs at someone's faults, making fun

Satisfaction in shortcomings - glad someone isn't "getting it right"

An evil report - spreading gossip or slander

## A Decision of My Heart:

*Dear Father, as an act of my will, I decide that from now on, with Your help, I choose not to be a tale bearer. I am no one's judge! God alone knows the hearts of men. I will leave the judging to Him! When we first meet someone, we get an opinion of them which can be good or not good. Help me, Lord, to keep the good and forget about the rest! Help me to speak only what is edifying about anyone. I have no reason for speaking negative about someone! Jesus does not broadcast my faults! Yay!*

# 1 Cor 13:6 <u>Love rejoices in the truth,</u> *aggressively advertising the good.*

**From God's point of view:** God is the Author and Finisher of Truth! Everything He thinks and speaks is nothing but True and Right. He has no variable of turning, no shadow, where truth and lies are mixed together. He loves and values us as His creation so much that He would never damage us by giving us falsehoods.

We see God in our natural world. Spectacular sunset sky pictures show us the beauty and majesty of God! The way sheep behave is very similar to us! A caterpillar turns into a butterfly, representing our new birth in Christ. *"The heavens declare the glory of God"* (Psalm 19:1). Isolated tribal people know there is a God when they look up! Creation advertises the truth of Who God is and what He is like. There is order in Creation, nothing "just happened."

**From my point of view:** The Bible is the best way of comprehending God's truth. I can confidently write my name in any verse, claiming the truth of it for my current situation. How liberating and wonderful that is! The truth really does set me free! Truth is also represented by the Person of Jesus. He is the Way, the Truth and the Life! Jesus knew the Father so well and His life (on earth) was an advertisement of how good the Father is to us!

## Definition of words:

Rejoices - exceedingly glad, heart happiness

Aggressively advertising - enthusiastically sharing truth

Good - beneficial, upright, helpful, blessing

## A Decision of My Heart:

*Dear Father, as an act of my will, I decide that from now on, with Your help, when a Bible verse is quickened to me, I will depend on it being God's perfect truth. God has put so many amazing promises in His Word and my part is to claim them to be true for me right now! He stands by His Word!*

*"Finally, brethren, whatever things are true, noble, just, pure, lovely, of good report, ... meditate on these things" (Philippians 4:8). It is easy to see the bad things in the world, but God wants us to advertise the good! How do we advertise the good? By living loved by God and loving others!*

# 1 Cor 13:7 <u>Love bears all things,</u> *defending and holding other people up.*

**From God's point of view:** How many times have you felt a little down and someone will say just the right thing to encourage you? Or a verse you read is just what you needed to lift you up? The Holy Spirit knows how to be the Lifter of our Heads! (Psalm 3:3). He is with us. He is our Counselor. He is our Helper. He prompts others to be there for us. Isn't He wonderful?!

Isaiah 43:1-3 tells us that when we go through a difficult time God knows our name (and everything about us!) and He says "You are Mine!" He is with us as we pass through the waters and walk through the fire. Because He said, "I am your Savior," we can relax and know we will not only get through this time of trial, but we will come out stronger, knowing His keeping power.

**From my point of view:** We are to follow the example of our Lord and act like Him. Since He bears with us, we can bear with others. Because we are defended and held up by the Lord, we can also do the same for others. It all starts with being thankful for how the Lord is treating us so lovingly and mercifully. Then we can extend that same love and mercy to others in word and deed.

## Definition of words:

Bears - holds up under pressure, takes the load to protect another

Defending - believes the best, speaking favorably for someone else

Holding people up - never gives up on anyone

## A Decision of My Heart:

*Dear Father, as an act of my will, I decide that from now on, with Your help, I will be open to helping someone in need. Remind me of how merciful You have been to me and give me the desire to pass those blessings along. Help me to give prayer support to ministries that bring help to the needy. May I learn about hurting ones, so I can pray for them. Current events and people mentioned on the news need the prayers of the saints!*

## 1 Cor 13:7 <u>Love believes the best</u> about others, credits them with good intentions and is not suspicious.

**From God's point of view:** When Jesus began His earthly ministry He chose twelve men to be with Him, to hear His teachings and learn the ways of the Kingdom of God. These men came from different backgrounds and occupations. One of these men, Matthew, was a mis-fit in the Jewish society of that day because he was a tax collector. And yet, Jesus believed the best about Matthew, even if the other disciples did not at first. Do you think Jesus believes the best about you? Matthew wrote one of The Gospels, preached in his homeland and led missionary campaigns in other nations. What amazing thing does Jesus see you doing in the future?

**From my point of view:** I am challenged by how Jesus welcomed Matthew into His band of men. Those were the chosen ones who would have full time intimacy with Him for three years. Does He invite me into the same full time relationship with Him? Even me? Does He believe the best about me? I think He does. What does He see in me that will some day produce something beneficial for the Kingdom? I don't know right now, but I can't help but think that His plans are amazing, way better than mine! Okay, Jesus, lead on! I will follow, just like Matthew did. And, just like his future was amazing, I am expecting my future to be amazing too! What about you? Do you think the Father waits until we are perfect before we can serve Him in some way?

## Definition of words:

Credits - commendation or honor given for some quality or action

Good intentions - good attitude, motive, action or purpose

Suspicious - to believe something to be evil or wrong

## A Decision of My Heart:

*Dear Father, as an act of my will, I decide that from now on, with Your help, I will believe that You are not always looking for me to mess up! You actually believe the best about me and also about every one of us!*

*Help me to see people like You do! I want to put on my "rose-colored glasses" when I'm with people, seeing only their strong points. I choose not to assign motives to anyone, only God knows what people are thinking and what is in their heart.*

# I Cor 13:7 <u>*Love hopes all things,*</u> *never giving up on people, but affirming their future.*

**From God's point of view:** Instead of becoming frustrated with difficult people, God has hope for them. He continues to find ways to draw them to Himself. He longs to have fellowship with every person, letting them know He has a better future for them. A future filled with peace and satisfaction. Even the thief on the cross knew in his heart that Jesus would not reject him. How did He know that? Because he could sense that Jesus loved him and would never give up on him, even to his dying breath.

**From my point of view:** I am amazed that God has not given up on me! Many times I haven't been happy with myself! It shows that an ingredient of Love is Hope. When He affirms our future, it says to us that better days are ahead and that His plans for us are all good. He puts hope in us to believe for positive things in coming days. Even if our circumstances don't change, He will help our faith to become strong, the Word to come alive and our joy to return. He refuses to give up on us!

*"Those who are loved by God, let his love continually pour from you to one another, because God is love"* (1 John 4:7 TPT). It's His perfect love for us,

in us and through us that enable us to love others and to love ourselves.

## Definition of words:

Hopes - longs for, expects, looking forward to

Affirming - confirm, uphold, express agreement

Future - a measurement of time, can be near or far from now

## A Decision of My Heart:

Dear *Father, as an act of my will, I decide that from now on, with Your help, I want to see people through the same lens as You use. What would You say to this person? What would You do for them or give to them? Is there a Scripture that would bless them? Show me Lord, how I should pray for this person? How can I encourage them? Help me to be the same kind of cheerleader for this person that You have been for me.*

*Help me remember that You will never give up on me and that You see a bright future ahead for me! That gives me so much encouragement.*

# 1 Cor 13:7 <u>Love endures all things,</u> *persevering and remaining loyal to the end.*

**From God's point of view:** Jesus showed us what Enduring Love is all about when He stayed on the cross. Jesus demonstrated His love for the Father by His obedience to the plan of salvation. Jesus demonstrated His love for sinful men by willfully giving up His own life so that even those who hate Him could be set free from the bondage of sin. He could have called on a legion of angels to rescue Himself and also put to death all of His accusers. The list of accusers would be long, as the jeering crowd would be included in that list. They cried out to Pilot to release Barabbas, a sinner. They chanted "crucify Him" referring to Jesus, in Whom was no sin. Even in the face of the rejection of His own people, Jesus stayed the course of Enduring Love.

**From my point of view:** God holds out hope for any person, no matter how lost in sin they are. Zacchaeus was a chief tax collector and he was rich. He wanted to see who Jesus was and climbed up in a tree. Jesus called out, "Zacchaeus, quickly come down, for I will stay at your house today!" (Luke 19:5). Can you imagine what went through the mind of Zacchaeus? (*How does He know my name? Wow! He knows my name!!! He wants to come to my house! MY house!! Doesn't He know how much I am hated? How I have cheated the* *people on their taxes?)* Jesus knew all of those things. He wanted Zacchaeus and us to know how vast His Enduring Love really is. Jesus refuses to give up on any person! His arms are open wide to receive even the person who thinks they are beyond help.

## Definition of words:

Endures - having patience, sticking it out, withstands

Persevering - persisting, holding on, dogged

Loyal - devoted, on one's side, resolutely faithful

## A Decision of My Heart:

*Dear Father, as an act of my will, I decide that from now on, with Your help, I want to see every person through the lens of Enduring Love, the same as Jesus does. Just as Zacchaeus was grateful for the Enduring Love of Jesus, so I also thank You, Lord, for having mercy on me! When I think of family and friends that are away from God, I remember the Enduring Love God has for them and I am encouraged to keep praying.*

# 1 Cor 13:8 <u>Love never fails,</u> never falls down, never disappoints.

**From God's point of view:** God IS Love! His very nature is to love. He can't be anything else but what He is! It is impossible for Him to stop loving! He can't stop helping, encouraging, providing for and blessing us because it would be unloving to stop doing those things. He cannot go against His nature, which is goodness, kindness, generosity and love.

**From my point of view:** I can always count on the promises of God in the Word to be true and available to me. I believe that God is love and love always does good for everyone. That's just how it is! God is good because God is love! God is kind and generous because that is how love acts. What an amazing comfort to know that God will never change! He is and always will be the same! That gives me great confidence to expect my prayers to be answered and my needs to be met.

Perhaps you live in a home where you are loved 24/7. Perhaps you have never known that kind of home. Either way, use your imagination to picture living with someone who loved you unconditionally. Someone who would encourage you, pray for you and help you when you need it. Someone who was always available to talk, to give a shoulder to cry on and is the best counselor ever. You DO live with that Someone! His name: Jesus.

## Definition of words:

Love - *agape* - wanting the highest and the best for someone

Fails, falls down - to fall short, unsuccessful, be let down

Disappoints - does not fulfill expectations or wishes

## A Decision of My Heart:

Dear *Father, as an act of my will, I decide that from now on, with Your help, I will count on You to meet my needs, whatever they may be. I trust You to be a Shield of Protection around me and a Place of Refuge to rest and be refreshed in. I am thankful that You are the Lifter of my Head when I am weary, confused or discouraged. I will boast that You are my Good Shepherd to lead and guide me, opening doors of opportunity for me. The blessing of the Lord has made me rich in so many ways! I am thankful that Your love for me never fails, falls down or disappoints. Your Name be glorified!*

# 1 Corinthians 13:4-8 Reference

1 Cor 13:4 through 1 Cor 13:8

All Definition of Words comes from dictionary.com.

# The Prodigal Son Story
## ~ Father's Love

When Jesus told this parable, His listeners knew that Jehovah was the One who had many rules to be followed. And, He could also be awesome to save them, as when He split the sea. The Israelites knew that Jehovah was holy and powerful! They did not know Him as a loving Father.

David knew the heart of God was merciful and full of lovingkindness, but even David did not address Him as "Father."

Luke 15:1-2 tells us that tax collectors and sinners liked to be with Jesus and hear His teachings. However, the Pharisees and scribes complained, saying, "This Man receives sinners and eats with them." They thought if Jesus were a holy man, He would know it is better to keep Himself separate from "sinners."

The attitude of the Pharisees prompted Jesus to tell a story about a new and very important aspect of Jehovah God's character. He is a Father who loves His creation. He loves them all, the saints and the sinners alike!

*Verses in bold type are from the New King James Version of Luke 15:11-32.*

*My thoughts are given in italic.*

## The Prodigal Son Story

*This story is taken from Luke 15:11-32 NKJV.*

**A certain man had two sons. And the younger of them said to his father, "Father, give me the portion of goods that falls to me." So he divided to them his livelihood.**

*In the light of Middle Eastern culture, it was a great offense for a son to ask his father for his inheritance. It would be the equivalent to saying, "I wish you were already dead." Those hearing this would have been shocked!*

*They would have been equally shocked to hear that the father gave his rebellious son what he asked for. That would have been unheard of!*

**And not many days after, the younger son gathered all together, journeyed to a far country, and there wasted his possessions with prodigal living.**

*It didn't take the younger son long to leave his father's house! He was ready to go! The sooner the better! He didn't even mind the long trip to a far country. He had heard stories of how wonderful it was there. Plenty of worldly pleasures to be enjoyed.*

*We are not told how long it took for him to waste all of his father's money with reckless and foolish living. Perhaps he also wanted to impress his friends by being overly generous toward them.*

**But when he had spent all, there arose a severe famine in that land, and he began to be in want. Then he went and joined himself to a citizen of that country, and he sent him into his fields to feed swine. And he would gladly have filled his stomach with the pods that the swine ate, and no one gave him anything.**

*With his money gone, the young man's "friends" were nowhere to be found! He must have felt very dejected and alone at that point. It sure didn't help any to have a severe famine in the land right then! Everything was working against him!*

*Good jobs were not readily available, so he took a job to feed pigs. Everyone listening to Jesus tell this story would know that pigs are considered "unclean" and Jews were prohibited from raising them. This would have been a degrading job for anyone, but especially for a Jew.*

*Evidently, he was not given enough money to buy food, or there was no food to buy because of the famine. He may have tried begging for food and was not given any. He even thought about eating the pig's food!*

**But when he came to himself, he said, "How many of my father's hired servants have bread enough and to spare, and I perish with hunger!"**

*The rebellious son "came to himself" and pondered his situation. He remembered the decisions he made to get himself into this predicament.*

*He reasoned that if he stayed where he was, he may even starve there! That was a scary prospect! His thoughts went back to his father's house, where he recalled there was plenty of food for the workers, even food left over! His mouth watered as he could almost smell the wonderful aroma that came from what was cooking and baking in the spacious kitchen at his father's house.*

**I will arise and go to my father, and will say to him, "Father, I have sinned against heaven and before you, and I am no longer worthy to be called your son. Make me like one of your hired servants."**

*The hardships the son faced brought him to see things differently. The ways of the world were not all they were cracked up to be! The thrill was gone! Reality had set in and it wasn't pretty.*

*The young man thought it through and decided to admit to his father that he was wrong. And, that he had sinned against heaven and in his father's sight. There was a deep-seated conviction that he would never be reconciled to his father because of his rebellious actions. He wouldn't even allow himself the thought that he would ever again be brought back into the family and be treated as a much-loved son. He had caused too much embarrassment and pain to his father. Too much water had gone under the bridge for any hope of reconciliation. The best he could hope for would be to work as a servant for his father.*

*It is interesting that when the younger son wanted his inheritance he said, "Father, give me." In the speech he is currently rehearsing, he uses the words - "Father, make me" a servant to you. This is a different boy talking! There is no more demanding his own way. He is speaking with respect to his father. He had even given up his* "rights" as a son in the house. That is brokenness and humility talking.

**And he arose and came to his father. But when he was still a great way off, his father saw him and had compassion, and ran and fell on his neck and kissed him.**

I remember the first time I read this part of the story as a new Christian. Tears ran down my face when I read that the father was watching for his wayward son and then actually ran to meet him, giving hugs and kisses! Picturing that kind of undeserved love really impacted me! It still does.

What was the younger son thinking when he saw his father running to him? Maybe that his father would be furious with him and even use physical force to teach him a lesson. Maybe the father would demand that he leave the property and not come back. He had disgraced the family enough!

That was not the case. Great compassion swelled up in the father's heart when he saw his son walking toward the house! He was so glad to see him coming that he actually ran to meet him! In those days, the man of the house would never run. Only servants ran. In order to run, a man would have to pull up his robe and his legs would show. That was just not done in their culture! It *seems the father set customs aside because of how excited he was to see his son coming home!*

*The son was hugged and kissed! Consider how the young man must have looked and smelled (being with pigs)! It took a lot of love from the father to give him such a passionate welcome! Love overcomes all!*

*How do you think the prodigal felt when he received such a welcome? How would you feel if it were you? What would happen to all the guilt and shame he carried in his heart? Would the power of love and forgiveness rock his world? In his wildest imagination, could he have pictured such a welcome? His eyes were being opened to the true nature of his father.*

**And the son said to him, "Father, I have sinned against heaven and in your sight, and am no longer worthy to be called your son."**

*Now the rehearsed speech begins. He reminds the father of his total unworthiness, that he is "not good enough." (Do we ever say that?) He doesn't think he could ever be good enough to be considered part of the family again. He had blown it! End of story.*

*The young man was about to go on with his prepared speech and ask for a job as a servant.*

*But the father interrupted; he was not listening. He started giving orders to the servants! The father was full of joy to have his son back!*

**But the father said to his servants, "Bring out the best robe and put it on him. And put a ring on his hand and sandals on his feet."**

*Each item the father gave to his son had significance. The robe would have been made of high-quality material with beautiful colors. Wealthy people would wear this kind, certainly not rebellious sons! The Scripture talks about a Robe of Righteousness. (Isaiah 61:10).*

*The ring was the seal of sonship and it gave the son the authority to transact business in the father's name. No more worries about food or anything else for that boy!*

*Servants went barefoot, so for the son to get a nice pair of sandals would have shown his status as a much-loved and cared-for son.*

**"And bring the fatted calf here and kill it, and let us eat and be merry; for this my son was dead, and is alive again; he was lost and is found." And they began to be merry.**

*Whoa! The father used the word "son!" The sweetest word the young man could ever hope to hear! Son! He could barely take in the meaning of that word, it seemed impossible. He remembered with shame all he had done. He was overcome with gratitude! For him to not get what he deserved, but to be treated with kindness, was nothing short of Grace and he knew it.*

*The father wasn't finished! He wanted a party! The kind of party that the whole village would be invited to. After all, the roasted, fatted calf would feed a lot of people! This was celebrating on a big scale!*

*The prodigal son was being enlightened into more of the father's true character. To think that his father would throw a big feast with music and dancing seemed impossible to him. He was amazed! He could hardly grasp the concept that the father loved him so much that he would arrange a party just for him! (Put yourself in the place of the prodigal. How would you feel if you heard that the Father wanted to throw a party just to celebrate that YOU came home to Him?)*

*Luke 15:10 tells us that the angels in heaven rejoice when one sinner repents! Someone who was dead in their sins and turns to God is made alive! Our heavenly Father loves to celebrate when we come to Him!*

**Now, his older son was in the field. And as he came and drew near to the house, he heard music and dancing. So he called one of the servants and asked what these things meant. And he said to him, your brother has come, and because he has received him safe and sound, your father has killed the fatted calf.**

*The older son is a picture of the Pharisees who were listening to this story told by Jesus. They believed that right standing with God depended on obedience to God's laws and commandments. This son was working for his father's love and acceptance.*

*When the older brother found out that the party was in honor of his younger brother, he was offended. Ever since his rebellious brother left home, he wrote him off as being a pathetic sinner who would never make anything decent or respectable out of his life. He felt he had every right to judge his younger brother so harshly.*

**But he was angry and would not go in. Therefore his father came out and pleaded with him.**

*The older son's anger came out of his deep-seated belief that we only get what we have worked for and deserve to get. He could not comprehend the idea of getting something good, like a party, when a whipping and being sent away was what his brother deserved by his sinful lifestyle.*

*It's interesting that the father came out of the house for both of his sons. He loved both of them, wanting each of them to enjoy the experience of being in his house, in close, loving fellowship with him.*

*The attitude of the older son showed that he did not know the depths of love his father had for him.*

**So he answered and said to his father, "Lo, these many years I have been serving you; I never transgressed your commandment at any time; and yet you never gave me a young goat, that I might make merry with my friends.**

*He goes on to remind his father what a wonderful son he has been; always faithful, never disobedient. Also, he blamed his father for never rewarding his hard work! It sounds like he was only interested in what he could get from his father, not in having a relationship with him.*

*The older brother tried to love his father perfectly by doing good works. It was a never-ending process! He didn't realize that he could simply relax and receive the perfect love the father had for him because he was a son.*

**"But as soon as this son of yours came, who has devoured your livelihood with harlots, you killed the fatted calf for him."**

*There are two contrasting attitudes in life - loving and judging. We are either doing one or the other all the time, there are no other options. The father in this story was doing all the loving and the older brother did the judging. The problem about judging is that it puts us in a position to be judged ourselves. (Matthew 7:1). God alone is the perfect Judge.*

**And he said to him, "Son, you are always with me and all that I have is yours. It was right that we should make merry and be glad, for your brother was dead and is alive again, and was lost and is found."**

*The older brother kept on working, with the hope that he would someday be told that he had become pleasing to his father. The truth is his father was already pleased with him!*

*Hear Him say, "All that I have is yours." This is an amazing word for all of us to ponder! Being a son or daughter of God means we can trust Him to provide for our needs. Awesome!*

*Or, are we trying to be worthy? Our Father celebrates that we are alive in Christ and part of His family! We can celebrate too!*

The father describes the prodigal as one who was dead, but now he is alive and back home. In some cultures, a family would hold a funeral, letting their friends know that their wayward son was no longer considered part of their family.

We all came to the Father when we were dead in our sins. He made us alive and we were born into His kingdom because of the death of His Son on our behalf.

Thank You, Jesus, for telling this awesome story about our heavenly Father who loves every one of us with Big Loves!

## *Lies and Truth*

**Lie:** The father could not or would not forgive the younger son.

**Truth:** The prodigal thought that his sins had accumulated to the point where there was no thought of receiving a pardon from his father. He had blown it completely! His "Very Good" father would never forgive his own "Very Bad" self! The best he could think of was to become a hired servant at the father's estate, living in the nearest town, simply receiving a paycheck so he could live comfortably.

The younger son did not know the true nature of his father. Some of us may have that same mindset. But, the truth is, Jesus took all of our sins, so we are not being judged for any of them! We are given Grace and Favor!

God is not holding our sins against us! *For I will be merciful to their unrighteousness, and their sins and their lawless deeds I will remember no more* (Hebrews 8:12).

## *Lies and Truth*

**Lie:** Our sin lessens our Father's love for us.

**Truth:** We may feel that God is far away from us, but that is only because our own heart condemns us. The Lord's heart is close by, wanting to help us through any trial or temptation. He loves us enough to be there to pick us up, wash us clean and give us the grace to start over with a clean slate. We may be fed up with ourselves at times, but God is never fed up with us!

In the Luke 15 story, the father knew that love is a powerful tool to win the heart of his prodigal son. *And above all things have fervent love for one another, for love will cover a multitude of sins.* (1 Peter 4:8).

Love can come dressed in different packages and the Holy Spirit is our best guide in how to love our prodigal. The bottom line is our son or daughter, spouse or friend, needs to know that, as a person, they are completely accepted and loved. Even when they know we don't love what they are doing or thinking because in the end it is hurtful for them. Would our friendly and loving attitude help them see things differently and give them the freedom to change for the better?

# *Lies and Truth*

**Lie:** We will not be pleasing to our Father unless we do works of service for Him.

**Truth:** God is not looking for servants, He's looking for sons and daughters! He wants a loving relationship with us! He wants a family!

Our motivation for serving is shown by responding in gratitude to the Father who poured out His love to us first. We soak in His love first and then go out and serve wherever He tells us.

Jesus spoke to the church at Ephesus in Revelation, Chapter Two. He complimented them for their hard work and perseverance and that they did not tolerate evil. They even endured trials and persecutions because of His Name and did not become discouraged. It really sounds like the perfect church, doesn't it? However, Jesus said they had abandoned the love they had for Him in the beginning. *Nevertheless I have this against you, that you have left your first love* (Revelation 2:4). Jesus is showing us what is really important to Him. Him loving us and us loving Him has to be our priority.

## *Lies and Truth*

**Lie:** When God looks at us He is checking to see if we are good Christians, representing Him well.

**Truth:** This powerful story of the prodigal shows us that Father God only saw one thing - He saw a son. He was looking at identity, not character.

Is our identity important? Yes, it matters a lot! We get our true identity from how our Father sees us. Only His view of us matters. The prodigal saw himself as an unworthy servant. The older brother's identity came from working hard so that some day he would be recognized and honored.

What is your primary identity? Are you a Much-Loved Son in the Father's family? A Much-Loved Daughter? Wouldn't you feel valuable and important having that position in His family? When a prince walks into a room, he carries himself with dignity, knowing who his father is and knowing the resources his father has. The prince knows he has a close relationship with his father, the king. It is the same with a princess. She knows she is special and that her father, the king, will always take good care of her! How do you see yourself? Are you Much-Loved? Are you Royalty?

## *Lies and Truth*

**Lie:** We should expect punishment for our sins. That's how life works!

**Truth:** The Pharisees would have said, "Of course, yes!" The fault-finding older brother would agree. He had no interest in seeing his lost brother come home to be restored. A characteristic of legalism is a lack of compassion.

The father showed grace to his prodigal son. He does that to us as well when we've messed up. It's so easy for us to expect, at the very least, that our Father God is disappointed in us when we are disappointed in ourselves. That's the time when we need to picture in our minds that smelly, dirty young man being held tightly in his father's arms and receiving many kisses!

Picture yourself as the prodigal, who went from wanting to steal food from pigs, to being seated at a banquet table as the guest of honor being served the finest food in the land! God's love accepts us as we are, but that love does not leave us the same way it found us. It's all about Grace. God's Love and Grace helped the prodigal to repent, to turn away from sin and want to be with his father. Love heals. Grace give us the power to change.

Wrong thinking and addictions do bring negative consequences with them. What we sow, we will reap. However, there are two things that influence negative or sinful sowing and reaping: Repentance and Grace. The prodigal is an example of one who repented. His thinking and his circumstances were changed by a merciful God. God is Good and He gives Grace to anyone who will humble themselves and call on His name for forgiveness and help.

## *Think About It*

What part does "humility" have to play in this story? Humility has been described as "thinking less of yourself." Actually, humility is really "thinking about yourself less!" Both of these sons had their focus on themselves! The older son thought he was too good, living right before God, to go to a party for his brother, a sinner. The Pharisees wondered why Jesus would eat with sinners. (Luke 5:30).

The younger son thought he was too bad to ever be forgiven or belong to such a righteous family. He had blown his chances for a happy life with Dad. Memory of his sins kept him bound in shame, just like having a ball and chain around his ankle. He let his past hinder him from knowing God's love.

Neither one of them knew the true heart of their father. One walked away to live in the world because deep down there is that nagging feeling of "I'm not good enough for a holy God." The other one became religious and worked to earn God's favor and blessings. All the time he was developing a heart that was more judgmental than loving.

Do you know people like those two sons? What if you encouraged both of these kinds of people to develop a close friendship with Father God? One attribute of God's character is mercy. It's easy to be humble when you are receiving love and mercy from God. There's no reason to run away or to try to earn favor when you know that *Through the Lord's mercies we are not consumed, because His compassions fail not* (Lamentations 3:22). God specializes in loving people into wholeness.

## *Think About It*

Two amazing statements the Father made to the older brother: *Son, you are always with me, and all that I have is yours* (Luke 15:31).

"You are always with me," tells me that our Father wants to be with us all day long. He wants a personal relationship. He actually enjoys our company! He wants to talk to us. Don't you think the One who makes planets knows a few things that might help us in our journey through life?! All we have to do is to be quiet and listen to that still small voice. Many times we hear Him when we are reading the Bible. He also loves to hear our voice. Sometimes our tears talk to Him. He understands it all.

"All that I have is yours." The word "all" is like a blank check! What does the Father have that He wants you to receive? How many promises are there in the Bible with your name on them? What God says in His Word is not only true, but it is true for you and me! We can enjoy what Father God has for us by putting our name on His promises!

# Think About It

The story of the Prodigal Son has symbolism concerning differences between the Old Testament (Old Covenant) and the New Testament (New Covenant).

The older brother represents the Old Covenant. He believed righteousness was earned by good works. A person had to prove that he loved God by trying to become as righteous as he could be, and by keeping The Law.

The prodigal is symbolic of all of us who come to the Lord "Just As I Am." The New Covenant is about grace and mercy and what it is like to be loved by the Father. *But God demonstrates His own love toward us, in that while we were still sinners, Christ died for us* (Romans 5:8).

Under the Old Covenant, there was a striving to do good. In the New Covenant there was the assurance of being in Jesus, who is good. The Old Covenant was about YOU cleaning up your act. YOU are on the throne of your heart. The New Covenant is about JESUS giving you the ability to do the right thing and JESUS being on the throne of your heart!

Religion will always point you to what you have or haven't done for God. The gospel will always point you to what Jesus did for you. One produces shame, guilt, and regret; the other produces love, joy, and peace.

## *Think About It*

The prodigal had a chance to repent (which means "change our mind") when he arrived at the father's house. He had pictured that the father would be angry with him. He thought he might even be turned away. That's why he hoped that he could be hired as a servant in his father's house. He said in his rehearsed speech: "Father, I have sinned against heaven and before you." That's the first indication of a "changed mind." The experience with the pigs had humbled him.

He was totally surprised and overwhelmed by the kindness that was lavished on him during that whole day. He "changed his mind" even more about what his father was like, a deeper repentance. The acceptance and care he felt coming from his father touched him deeply. As a result he viewed his father as one who had extraordinary love and extravagant mercy.

When we are treated better than we deserve, our hearts become soft. When we are being judged, our defenses usually rise up!

Later that day the young man had a bath, a nice lunch and a beautiful robe to wear. By the time he had his scraggly beard and matted hair washed and trimmed, he was probably pretty handsome!

He could smell the savory meat roasting and see the servants decorating for the party. Pretty soon the musicians arrived and it sunk deep into his heart that this whole occasion was in honor of him - just him! He wept with gratitude and joy. He was home. He knew he would never want to leave the father's house again.

## *Think About It*

What do you and I believe about the character of Father God? Do we think He is amazingly good? Do we picture Him as quick to forgive, overflowing with love for us? Does He always want to bless us - or is He watching to see if we are doing the right things?

Can you imagine that on your worst day the Father would RUN to be with you, to hug and kiss you? Can I imagine that? If it is hard to imagine that, do we need to "change our minds" about who the Father really is for us?

## *Think About It*

The prodigal was away from home in a far country. The older brother was away from the enjoyment of his home, even while he remained at home. Did the older son know or care about the privileges that were his? He could have had fellowship with the father and enjoyed anything belonging to the father. All of this privilege was waiting for and offered to him, but not received. He lived in his own far country.

Two things separate us from fellowship with God - sin and unbelief. The prodigal had sin and the older brother had unbelief. The older son could not believe in Grace. To him, everything was accomplished by merit. Both sin and unbelief cause us to be the ones to back away from being close with our Father. We think God will not tolerate sin or unbelief.

The Father, on the other hand, does not see sin or unbelief as barriers. He doesn't keep His distance from us. He is like the father in the story, watching and waiting for the younger son to come back, and also leaving the party to come out and talk with the older son. The father's heart was the opposite of being aloof and stand-offish. He left the house and came TO each son with love and mercy in his heart. That's how our Father treats us.

## *Think About It - Use Your Imagination*

The Homecoming Party was over and the younger son was settling into life with his father. Could coming to the father represent how we come to the Lord with our sinful nature and then become born again, getting a new heart, a new spirit, a new start in life? The best "do-over" ever!

The next steps for this son would be to develop new thinking patterns, new ways to do life. His father was the best teacher and guide. He found that being with the father was such a pleasure for him. He was daily learning about how amazing his father was and also experiencing the wonderful gifts the father gave him, like the gift of peace. (John 14:27).

One day, the younger son heard the father tell him how much He enjoyed his company! That was completely unexpected, since he knew he slipped back into old language and thought patterns once in awhile. He wasn't anywhere near "perfect" like his father was, even though he wanted to be. He didn't understand how he could bring pleasure to his father, that sounded unreal to him! But he knew the father always said only what was truth, so he told his heart to believe and receive that truth.

The more time the younger son spent with the father, the more he wanted to say Thank You for everything! He spent time in quiet adoration. He found himself thinking more and more about how good and kind the Father was and sometimes that would even bring him to tears.

If we don't look forward to times of being with the Father, is it because we don't think He loves us unconditionally? Time to meditate on Father Loves Me scriptures! Do you or I think our faults and failings can separate us from the love of God? Not happening! (Romans 8:38-39). He loves us! Period!

What about you? What about me? Do we realize that we can choose to enjoy our Father's company, like the younger son did? It is being in His sweet presence that makes us want to do anything He asks us to do. Serving Him becomes a joy. Time spent in receiving His love and nearness is so beneficial to us that it becomes a "must have" in our lives. When we make being with God a priority, we can tell our hearts that He also enjoys being with us.

# *In Conclusion*

Dear Heavenly Father,

When I'm acting like the Older Brother, trying to make my identity about what I am doing, I repent. I choose to spend time with You, soaking in Your love, giving You my cares and enjoying Your company. Then, after I am filled with the joy of being Your daughter, I will go into the fields.

When I'm acting like the Younger Son, wanting what You can give to me and not wanting You alone, I repent. I am sorry for the times I have not been quickly obedient and went my own way. I choose to do life with You.

I love You Father,
Karen Marie

# Fruit of the Spirit ~ Love Manifested

*If you and I lived in the time of Jesus and were able to follow Him around, we would see every one of the fruits of the Spirit manifested in His life. Can you imagine Him laughing for joy at a great healing miracle? Like an audible celebration of the Father's Love and Power! Or gently taking a child on His lap and blessing him/her? Jesus treated all of His disciples with patience. Yes, Judas too. Jesus gave correction because He loved everyone He spoke with, like the Pharisees. He wanted them to see the truth. He loved them enough to confront.*

*Romans 5:5 tells us that the Holy Spirit was given to us as a Gift when we were born again. He brought His fruit with Him when He came to live in us! Count on already having all of the nine fruits! We see them ripen and mature inside of us each time we choose to use them.*

# LOVE

*We love Him because He first loved us* (1 John 4:19).

We are first loved by God. We respond to that love and receive it into our hearts. Then we give away His love to the world. The God-kind of love does not expect anything back in return, not even a thank you! God loves us simply because that's Who He is and what He does! His love was planted inside of us when we were born again. We can love freely like He does.

*...The love of God has been poured out in our hearts by the Holy Spirit who was given to us* (Romans 5:5).

This is a great verse because it explains how I can love someone I find hard to love. First, it describes God's powerful love, not my meager attempt at love. Second, it is the Holy Spirit (who is a gift to me, not deserved), who actually enables God's love to flow through my heart to someone else. Third, my part is to choose to let that love flow happen. It says, *poured out* - I decide if I want it to be poured out of my heart or not. This verse tells how we can choose to love, even when we don't feel loving toward someone.

*But above all these things put on love, which is the bond of perfection* (Colossians 3:14).

The key is to "put on" love the same way we would put on our clothes. We go to the closet, decide what to wear and then dress ourselves. We don't get dressed by accident, it always involves a decision. We can go to our "heart closet" and choose to dress ourself with God's unconditional love.

We can also dress ourselves with resentment or anger; it's up to us. We do have the power of God within us to refuse to let those negative emotions rule us! We can see others the same way Jesus sees us. He sees us as a much-loved person. We can choose to see others through that same lens.

*Keep yourselves in the love of God...* (Jude 21). Fight off feelings of offense and allow the Lord to heal those heart hurts. *He wants to do that!* He's the best Heart Healer there is! Say Romans 5:5 and make it personal for you.

The world sees love as being something we feel. God's love is something we choose to use. Emotions will come later. We decide to give love, kindness and mercy, simply because that is what our Lord has given to us! Jesus wants to strengthen our hearts! Lean on Him when it's hard to love. *I can do all things through Christ who strengthens me* (Philippians 4:13).

# JOY

*My brethren, count it all joy when you fall into various trials* (James 1:2).

Paul mentions joy, rejoice or rejoicing 18 times in the book of Philippians! This is amazing, considering he wrote that letter while in jail. He proves to us that the Spirit's fruit of joy does not depend on outward conditions or what we are suffering. It's more than the happiness we feel when things are good. It's a supernatural grace that enables us to endure through rough times. When we use God's joy, it becomes our strength! (Nehemiah 8:10).

Paul tells us to *rejoice in the Lord always* (Philippians 4:4). We can obey that because our joy is <u>in the Lord;</u> who He is and what He will lovingly do for us.

How do we learn to count it all joy?
> Know the Spirit came to live in us when we were born again.
> He brought all of His fruit with Him to abide continually in us.
> Count on the fruit of joy to be resident in us and available now.
> Thank God for giving us the supernatural fruit of joy!

How can we maintain a lifestyle of joy?
> By knowing our God loves us and is bigger than our problems.

Don't focus on the problem, focus on what
God will do.

Know that God will always be our Keeper in
every situation.

By making Praise and Worship a lifestyle.

Did Jesus have joy?

*...Therefore God, Your God, has anointed You
with the oil of gladness more than Your
companions* (Hebrews 1:9).

Jesus found satisfaction in doing the will of
His Father. (John 4:34).

Jesus heard reports from the 70 who were
sent out and His reaction was to rejoice
in the Spirit! (Luke 10:21).

*Though the fig tree may not blossom, nor fruit
be on the vines, though the labor of the olive fail,
and the fields yield no food; though the flock may
be cut off from the fold, and there be no herd in
the stalls, yet I will rejoice in the Lord, I will joy in
the God of my salvation* (Habakkuk 3:17-18). The
prophet encouraged his people to not focus on
the lack, but on God who gives joy and salvation.
Habakkuk ministered in Judah during a difficult
time. He saw God as One who was able to supply
all of their needs. Do we?

*These things I have spoken to you, that My joy
may remain in you, and that your joy may be full*
(John 15:11). That sounds good, doesn't it?!

# PEACE

*Great peace have those who love Your law, and nothing causes them to stumble* (Psalm 119:165).

When we love God's law and gain understanding from the truth of His Word, we receive peace. We grow in peace effortlessly, simply by loving to read and digest what God has to say to us in His Word. No stumbling for us!

*Grace and peace be multiplied to you in the knowledge of God and of Jesus our Lord* (2 Peter 1:2).

When we really have heart knowledge of the love and grace the Godhead has toward us, it brings peace. How do you picture God? One who sees our faults? No, He sees each one of us as someone He wants to love and care for! Knowing and believing that gives us peace and rest.

Benefits of Living in Peace

*...and the peace of God, which surpasses all understanding, will* <u>*guard your hearts and minds*</u> *through Christ Jesus* (Philippians 4:7).

God's peace on the inside of us helps us to make right decisions. When we are thinking about making a wrong turn, we lose our peace. Peace floods our soul when we're on the right track and that gives us assurance.

Peace dominates over fear and anxiety! Those past habits have no place in our hearts anymore! We are not moved by upsetting circumstances. When we rely on the Holy Spirit's supernatural fruit of peace inside of us, we have the power to stay calm and stable, even while facing difficulties. *You will keep him in perfect peace, whose mind is stayed on You, because he trusts in You* (Isaiah 26:3). God is way bigger than any problem we can have!

Choose Peace to Govern all Relationships

*If it is possible, as much as depends on you, live peaceably with all men* (Romans 12:18). *Blessed are the peacemakers, for they shall be called sons of God* (Matthew 5:9).

*Peace I leave with you, My peace I give to you; not as the world gives do I give to you. Let not your heart be troubled, neither let it be afraid* (John 14:27). Open your heart to the gift of peace. Close your heart to problems and fear. Give your cares to Jesus and then enjoy His calmness and rest. We can choose what we focus on. Find a good promise verse and stand on it!

# PATIENCE

*Now may the God of patience and comfort grant you to be like-minded toward one another, according to Christ Jesus* (Romans 15:5). To learn patience, we must go through different situations, and that takes T.I.M.E. No one will totally master this fruit after a weekend seminar teaching!

When our cup is bumped, what comes out? New situations can be a stepping stone or a stumbling block in our journey to learn patience. It's our choice.

Benefits of Having Patience
> We are happier when we are patient, even with our sandpaper people.
> It's easier to forgive and forget when our feelings get hurt.
> Relationships are richer, people want to be with us, life is good!

Results from Being Impatient
> Poor relationships result from being short with people, annoyed.
> Losing a job or position can come from not controlling our temper.
> Not finishing a project or schooling can cost us later in life.

Things to Watch For:
> Most times it is not the big irritations that we lose patience over. It's the small, but frequent,

things that cause us to fume. These are the little foxes, ones the enemy throws at us to wear us down. Stay aware, so we can resist those negative reactions before they pile up and overwhelm us. And, we must not forget to be patient with ourselves!

## Jesus is Patient and He Lives Inside of Us!

Jesus knew that for most of us, patience does not come naturally! We don't have what it takes in ourselves to be patient. That's why we need supernatural help from the Lord who lives inside! Reflect on how Jesus lived His whole life in "patience mode!" Especially on the last day of His life.

Instead of saying, "I need" patience, what if we said, "I have" patience. We just need to count on it and use it! Lord Jesus, You are my Source and Strength to display patience, endurance and love! I count on You in me.

*The Lord is my strength and my shield; my heart trusted in Him, and I am helped; therefore my heart greatly rejoices, and with my song I will praise Him* (Psalm 28:7). *The Lord will give strength to His people; the Lord will bless His people with peace* (Psalm 29:11). Replace "His people" with your name. That verse is true of you! Say the verse out loud with your name!

# KINDNESS

*And be kind to one another, tenderhearted, forgiving one another, even as God in Christ forgave you* (Ephesians 4:32).

Each fruit of the Spirit comes to our heart in seed form to begin with. We cultivate it and make it grow by being obedient to what the Word of God says to us about it. We also stay sensitive to the Holy Spirit. They are His Fruit! He knows all about them and how He helps us make them grow!

God Himself Liberally Gives us His Kindness

*Praise the Lord, all you Gentiles! Laud Him, all you peoples! For His merciful kindness is great toward us...* (Psalm 117:1-2).

*For the mountains shall depart and the hills be removed, but My kindness shall not depart from you...* (Isaiah 54:10).

Can you think of a way God has shown you kindness? The verses above tell us that God initiates the showing of kindness in some way. He is not asking us to deserve it first. Actually, we often do kind things for others because we have benefitted by God's kindness ourselves.

A person that carries a tender and forgiving heart attitude does not look at the faults of others.

It's nice to be around such a person, don't you think? People are attracted to kindness. They were attracted to the Kind Jesus.

Demonstrate the Fruit of Kindness by Giving

*...But he who has mercy on the poor, happy is he* (Proverbs 14:21). *He who gives to the poor will not lack* (Proverbs 28:27).

*And let us not grow weary while doing good, for in due season we shall reap if we do not lose heart. Therefore, as we have opportunity, let us do good to all, especially to those who are in the household of faith* (Galatians 6:9-10). A kind word or deed is how we show love to our faith family.

Even a small act of kindness can bring a big amount of encouragement to a person. Have you ever felt encouraged when someone says they are praying for you? Has a friend ever given you a small gift or meaningful card for no special reason? Perhaps a friendly phone call? How did that make you feel?

Kindness is powerful! People are attracted to the Jesus in us when we are kind. Ask God to give you an idea of how to bless someone. It's fun to make plans to encourage someone! Spread the kindness! It will come back to you!

# GOODNESS

*What good thing shall I do that I may have eternal life?* The rich young ruler asked Jesus this question in Matthew 19:16. Since he was a child, he had kept the Ten Commandments, so he hoped to have earned the right to experience eternal life though his obedience.

Jesus told him to sell everything and follow Him. He could not do that. By making an idol of wealth, he broke the very first Commandment, *You shall have no other gods before Me* (Exodus 20:3). Jesus exposed his heart condition so he would realize he was not good! The young man needed the Grace of God, not keeping the Law, to have eternal life.

*You are good, and do good* (Psalm 119:68). The fruit of Goodness is a part of the nature and character of God. This is who He is and how He acts!

Goodness is also clearly seen in the life of Jesus. He *went about doing good* (Acts 10:38). Goodness is Love In Action! Jesus was good and He did good! He touched people; He went to their bedside. Jesus shows us how to be hands-on and personal when helping people. Jesus went out of His way to help. He didn't expect someone else to do it, or wait until it was convenient.

Do you think it may be the small things we do to help or encourage someone that count with God? The things no one else knows about? I think so.

Simply being quietly obedient to those promptings from the Holy Spirit pleases God.

Goodness is first who we are. Then, as a result of knowing who we are, it is what we do. If you and I are trying (without God's help) to be good, we are just like the rich young ruler who wanted eternal life because he tried to earned it. The truth is, Jesus earned it for us! *For He made Him who knew no sin to be sin for us, that we might become the righteousness of God in Him* (2 Corinthians 5:21). God has made us good; now we can act like it!

Edible fruit growing in an orchard has to be watched over and cared for. Spiritual fruit ripens the same way as natural fruit. We gradually develop in the Spirit's fruit of Goodness because He is our Teacher and Enabler!

*Either make the tree good and its fruit good, or else make the tree bad and its fruit bad, for a tree is known by its fruit... For out of the abundance of the heart the mouth speaks. A GOOD man out of the GOOD treasure of his heart brings forth GOOD things, and an evil man out of the evil treasure brings forth evil things* (Matthew 12:33-35). When we walk in the Spirit, our eyes are open to see needs and our hearts are moved to meet those needs.

# FAITHFULNESS

Hebrews 11:6 tells us, ...*he who comes to God must <u>believe that He is</u>, and that <u>He is a rewarder</u> of those who diligently seek Him.* God is faithful to us and has put His nature inside of us. We can be faithful because of His faithfulness in us. We seek Him because He is us our Rewarder!

How Faithfulness is Developed in Us for a Task

God taught faithfulness to Joshua. Read Joshua 1:1-9.

* God gave <u>Instructions</u> - Arise and go! You and all the people.
* Then <u>Promises</u> - I'm giving you the land, you won't fail, I will be with you!
* More <u>Instructions</u> - Be strong and of good courage, speak out the words in the Book of the Law, meditate in it day and night *so that* you will know what to do, Joshua. For *then* you will make your way prosperous and *then* you will have good success.
* A <u>Command and a Promise</u> - Be strong and of good courage, do not be afraid. Joshua was also assured that God would be with him to help.

With each instruction God gave, there was the promise of His help. It's the same with us. God helps us to be faithful in any task He calls us to. God repeated His instructions and His promises to Joshua, just like He does with us. God had a job for Joshua to do. He also has a job for you and me to do!

Don't be surprised if, when you are faithful in the little things, God will give you bigger things to do for Him! Joshua proved himself faithful as an assistant to Moses long before God gave him full leadership.

How Faithfulness is Developed in Us when Using Our Talents - Read The Parable of The Talents in Matthew 25:14-30.

What are some of the resources or abilities God gave you to use in His Kingdom? He created you for a purpose and has equipped you with gifts.

From this parable, we learn the following truths:

* If you use what is given to you, you will gain more.
* If you fail to use what is given to you, you will lose what you were given!

Just like in the parable, we have a returning Master who will be our Judge.

On Judgment Day, we want to hear, "Well done, good and faithful servant!" We are not equal in talents, but we can be equal in our faithfulness to use the ones we have been given.

# GENTLENESS

Jesus said, *Take My yoke upon you, and learn from Me, for I am gentle and lowly in heart, and you will find rest for your souls* (Matthew 11:29).

When we are yoked with Him, we take on His gentleness and our soul finds rest. Jesus was not only gentle and lowly in heart, He was also powerful and able to do miracles! Gentleness and a similar word - meekness, do not mean weakness! These two words actually mean strength under control. Being yoked with Jesus means we can partner with Him in gentleness and power.

How to Develop Gentleness

> Allow the Spirit of God to work in our inner character. Ask His help!

> Realize that we are to be *gentle, showing all humility to all men.* We were once disobedient and deceived, pursuing pleasures. But then *the kindness and love of God our Savior* gave us mercy and salvation. (Titus 3:2-5). We give away what we've been given.

Benefits of Being a Gentle Person

> We are being conformed to the image of Jesus. People are comfortable around us, knowing we aren't harsh, abrasive.

Like a wild horse has been "gentled" we are sensitive, obedient to God.

To have real beauty: *Do not let your adornment be merely outward - arranging the hair, wearing gold, or putting on fine apparel, rather let it be the hidden person of the heart, with the incorruptible beauty of a gentle and quiet spirit, which is very precious in the sight of God* (1 Peter 3:3-4).

Paul instructed Timothy that one of the qualifications of a church Leader was to be gentle, not quarrelsome. (1 Timothy 3:3). Paul wanted men in leadership to have good character, ones who were fair and considerate.

Philippians 4:5 instructs us to *Let your gentleness be known to all men. The Lord is at hand.* In other words, let your kind and peaceful attitude be seen in every relationship. The Lord is nearby us now and is coming in glory!

James asks the question, *Who is wise and understanding among you? Let him show by good conduct that his works are done in the meekness of wisdom. For where envy and self-seeking exist, confusion and every evil thing are there. But the wisdom that is from above is first pure, then peaceable, gentle, willing to yield, full of mercy...* (James 3:13,16-17).

# SELF-CONTROL

*Whoever has no rule over his own spirit is like a city broken down, without walls* (Proverbs 25:28).

Jesus showed us how to live with restraints. He would go to solitary places to pray, sometimes very early in the morning and even all night, missing sleep. He would speak to crowds of people even when He must have been tired or thirsty and hungry. He limited Himself to simply accomplishing the will of His Father. That is what living with restraints looks like. Jesus lived with His self-life surrendered to the Father. We can do the same. It just takes practice.

We can gradually learn to be like Him. The early church people were given the name "Christian" which means "little Christs." When we live out the fruits of the Spirit, we are like Him! God's grace is always there to help us to grow in godliness and overcome selfish habits.

We are to bring *every thought into captivity to the obedience of Christ* (2 Corinthians 10:5). We are to stop every disobedient thought, those going contrary to the ways of God, and not allow them to dominate our thinking. Cast down negative thoughts that challenge our identity in Christ. We must hold to the truths of who we are in Christ and what we have in Him.

Self-control means we have power to control ourselves, our passions and desires. When we over-work, over-worry, over-eat, not get enough sleep, or way too much sleep, we are not maintaining a life that is moderate and balanced. The Holy Spirit within us was given to help us be wise and disciplined for the sake of our health, and to be able to serve God well.

Every Olympic athlete and professional sports person has had to use self-control when training to become excellent at what they do. It's the same with businessmen, teachers, accountants, doctors and garage mechanics to name just a few. It makes a difference when we are at our best!

We really can't change ourselves without God's help. We need that inward grace and strength working through us. Lord Holy Spirit, change me, I pray. Help me to cooperate with You. I want to be able to control my thoughts, my mouth and my actions so that only Your love comes through.

*For as he thinks in his heart, so is he* (Proverbs 23:7). *A soft answer turns away wrath, but a harsh word stirs up anger* (Proverbs 15:1). Self-control is a powerful fruit! What a difference it makes in a life! *A man will be satisfied with good by the fruit of his mouth* (Proverbs 12:14).

Printed in the United States
by Baker & Taylor Publisher Services